SCOTTISH WOMEN'S FICTION, 1920s TO 1960s:
JOURNEYS INTO BEING

SCOTTISH WOMEN'S FICTION, 1920s TO 1960s: JOURNEYS INTO BEING

Edited by
Carol Anderson
and
Aileen Christianson

Tuckwell Press

Published in Great Britain in 2000
Tuckwell Press Ltd
The Mill House
Phantassie
East Linton
East Lothian
EH40 3DG

The publishers acknowledge subsidy
from the Scottish Arts Council towards
the publication of this volume.

ISBN 1 86232 082 9

Typset by Cairns Craig
Printed by The Cromwell Press
Trowbridge, Wiltshire.

CONTENTS

Acknowledgements   6
Introduction
    Carol Anderson and Aileen Christianson   7
'Behold I make all things new': Catherine Carswell
  and the Visual Arts
    Carol Anderson   20
Feminine Space, Feminine Sentence:
  Rebecca West's *The Judge*
    Carol Anderson   32
Boundaries and Transgression in
  Nan Shepherd's *The Quarry Wood*
    Gillian Carter   47
'Journey into Being': Nan Shepherd's *The Weatherhouse*
    Alison Lumsden   59
The Location of Magic in Naomi Mitchison's
  The Corn King and the Spring Queen
    Margaret Elphinstone   72
Dreaming Realities: Willa Muir's *Imagined Corners*
    Aileen Christianson   84
'An ordinary little girl': Willa Muir's *Mrs Ritchie*
    Beth Dickson   97
Poetic Narrative in Nancy Brysson Morrison's *The Gowk Storm*
    Margery Palmer McCulloch   109
Borderlines: Jessie Kesson's *The White Bird Passes*
    Glenda Norquay   122
Certainty and Unease in Muriel Spark's *The Ballad of Peckham Rye*
    Aileen Christianson   135
A Far Cry from the Kailyard: Jessie Kesson's *Glitter of Mica*
    Isobel Murray   147
A Select Bibliography of Scottish Women Writers, 1920s to 1960s
    Jennie Rubio   158
Further Reading   166
Contributors   173
Index   175

Acknowledgments

The editors and publisher wish to record their thanks to the following for permission to quote from the works of these writers: the late John Carswell for Catherine Carswell; the estate of Jessie Kesson and John Johnson Authors' Agents for Jessie Kesson; the late Naomi Mitchison for her works; Dr Elizabeth Michie for Nancy Brysson Morrison; Ethel E. Ross and the National Library of Scotland for Willa Muir; John Clouston for Nan Shepherd; Dame Muriel Spark for her works; Peters Fraser and Dunlop Group, Literary Agents, for Rebecca West.

The editors also wish to thank all the contributors to this volume. Further thanks for particular help and support are due to Helen Boden, Cairns Craig, Norma Clarke, Joyce Dietz, Jean Raulin Frere, Katherine Gordon, Jill Higginson, Alison Lumsden, Margery Palmer McCulloch, Isobel Murray, Glenda Norquay, Jan Pilditch and Eilidh Whiteford.

They would also like to thank the Faculty of Arts, Edinburgh University, for study leave and a grant from the Researches Expenses Fund, and the Faculty of Arts, Glasgow University, for study leave and research funding.

Introduction

Carol Anderson and Aileen Christianson

There has been a striking expansion in the reading and study of Scottish women's writing in recent years. The republication of novels by Catherine Carswell, Willa Muir, Nancy Brysson Morrison, Nan Shepherd and others has proved a major impetus for the reappraisal of writers whose work had been out of print and long neglected. Critics such as Elaine Showalter writing in the seventies, discussing mainly English and American fiction, drew attention to the value and interest of women's writing, and argued for the idea of women's traditions in fiction. To find that Scotland also had women writers whose works had disappeared has been exciting for many readers, including critics, and has led to the production of this volume, focusing on twentieth century novels. The reappearance of 'lost' women novelists has not only expanded the Scottish literary 'canon', it has brought new contexts in which to read the work of writers like Rebecca West or Naomi Mitchison, already well-known, if still insufficiently discussed. The writers and texts examined here show a diversity of regional backgrounds, of position within Scottish traditions, of narrative methods, and of themes. This collection of essays, with its detailed analyses of individual texts (discussed chronologically, in order of their first publication), conveys that difference and diversity that we find so stimulating.

The complexity and plurality of the work of Scottish women writers in the twentieth century is suggested by our title, drawn from Nan Shepherd's late non-fiction work *The Living Mountain*, a meditation on her experience of the Scottish hills. She concludes that the 'journey' is not only into the life of the mountain but into the self:

> I believe that I now understand in some small measure why the Buddhist goes on pilgrimage to a mountain. The journey is itself part of the technique by which the god is sought. It is a journey into Being (84).

By pluralising the 'journey' in our title, we hope to suggest the variety
and range of experiences that these women writers explore: the spiritual
dimensions as well as the material, the social and historical as well as the
metaphysical.

The emphasis on detailed readings of particular texts is intended as a
development from the already existing work, often very useful, on Scottish
women writers in collections of essays (for instance Gonda, Whyte) and in
scattered articles in journals and books. Work on Scottish women's writing
up to now has tended to examine groups of particular women writers, to
consider some of the writers briefly as small units in a larger context, or,
in Gifford and McMillan, to attempt coverage of a very wide number of
Scottish women writers. This volume seeks both to offer a close examination of particular works and to provide a sense of the variety to be found
in women's writing in Scotland in the twentieth century. The application of
feminist and other critical theories has also opened up a plurality of possible
approaches to these writers.

The writers we have chosen for consideration were all born in the late
nineteenth or early twentieth centuries:

> Catherine Carswell, born 1879
> Willa Muir, born 1890
> Rebecca West, born 1892
> Nan Shepherd, born 1893
> Naomi Mitchison, born 1897
> Nancy Brysson Morrison, born 1907
> Jessie Kesson, born 1916
> Muriel Spark, born 1918.

Born within a forty year period, these writers offer a sense of the growth
and development of writing by women in Scotland this century, from the
twenties to the sixties. A concern with female identity runs throughout
their works; in most there is some exploration of women's sexuality, of
relationships with other women and with men, of motherhood, and of the
experience of exclusion from institutions and from social power. Most have
been touched by some degree of feminist awareness, all of them having lived
through the changes wrought by early twentieth century feminism.

Writers such as Carswell and West offer a powerful sense of the changing experience and perceptions of women in the early twenties in Scotland,
while Shepherd, Muir, Mitchison (as represented here) and Morrison all
write from the perspective of the later twenties and thirties. Spark and

Kesson, born in the early years of the century, both matured late as writers. Writing in the fifties and sixties, they present a sense of continuity, as well as forming a bridge into more recent writing by women.

We have chosen to focus on the novel (rather than other prose forms or poetry) because we feel it forms a particularly accessible and rich strand in Scottish literature in this period. The choice of texts has been influenced by availability; Scottish texts tend to come in and out of print, as do those by women. During the planning of this collection, some of our chosen novels reappeared in print (eg *Mrs Ritchie*), encouraging us to include them, although unfortunately we lost others (eg *Glitter of Mica*). The choice of the novel as our focus and the constraints of space have meant some exclusions: for example, some novels by our chosen authors and the interesting work in the short story done not only by Kesson and Spark but also by others not looked at in any detail here, such as Lorna Moon and Dorothy K. Haynes. The interests of our contributors have helped shape the volume too; this book is not intended to construct a 'canon' of women's writing, but to suggest the importance of various novels, some less well known than others, and to make connections between them. We have deliberately chosen to focus on women working in the earlier and middle years of this century and not on the younger Scottish women writers such as Janice Galloway and A.L.Kennedy who have matured in a different cultural climate and therefore are more usefully assessed in a post-sixties context.

While these writers share certain kinds of cultural background and experience which affect their work, they do not share one generalised voice or viewpoint, offering instead a wide range of approaches. As with other Scottish writers, male and female, the question of Scotland is often addressed through region rather than nation. Willa Muir and Jessie Kesson, for instance, address questions of regional rather then national identity self-consciously; Mitchison, on the other hand, turns rather to the creation of other settings and times that may nevertheless enable her to deal with contemporary political issues not specific to Scotland, although relevant to it, and growing in complex ways out of Mitchison's own engagement with Scottish identity. Shepherd and Morrison, although grappling with aspects of Scottish identity, do not foreground these in their work. Spark's novels are mainly set outwith Scotland and yet she writes from within a recognisably Scottish tradition.

It is important to note as well that the writers work from their experience of different parts of Scotland: Carswell in the west, Kesson and Shepherd in the north-east; Morrison dealing with life in a Highland parish, and Muir in her small east coast town. We want to emphasise the regional identity of their works; to set novels of urban life (Carswell in Glasgow, West in Edinburgh, Spark in London) alongside those with rural settings. The question of class is complex, too, especially when considering such different environments. The novels looked at in this volume show the intricacies of class position: the small town deprivations of *A White Bird Passes*, the stifling bourgeois world of the small town of Calderwick in *Imagined Corners*, the upper working and lower middle class structures of Peckham Rye, arguably a small town despite being part of London, in *The Ballad of Peckham Rye*. All the novels show the ways in which class and gender interact and complicate each other: for example, West's single mother and her daughter in *The Judge* struggle with gentility and poverty in Edinburgh, while Kesson's unconventional Sue Tatt in *Glitter of Mica* is the character most harshly excluded from the small, narrow community of Caldwell.

We do not see these writers as coming out of any one single and unified 'Scottish tradition'. There is a complex interweaving of traditions and influences in the works of our chosen writers that needs to be understood within a larger context. There is a self-consciousness and, sometimes, anxiety about national identity often discernible in the work of Scottish writers (or writers of Scottish formation) and this is frequently related to a conscious engagement with aspects of Scottish culture: the oral tradition (ballad, song and storytelling) as well as a variety of male literary forebears, such as Burns, Scott, Hogg and Stevenson. Those writers who explore rural and small town life respond critically to the oversimplified pictures presented by the Kailyard writing of the late nineteenth century, adapting and developing for their own purposes the anti-Kailyard stance of George Douglas Brown. The two most recent writers are in an important sense separated from the others as they did not begin publishing until after the second world war. Spark also seems distinct because of her perceived role as an early postmodernist. Yet both Kesson and Spark, apparently such different kinds of writers, are linked to the earlier writers, as well as to each other, through their use of the ballad tradition and their tightly focused examination of small and well defined communities.

The complexity of Scottish writing becomes even more apparent when gender is brought into play. Because of the way in which their published works went out of print and disappeared (as with women writers more widely), it has been difficult until recently to talk securely of any specific 'Scottish women's tradition'. The women writers of the twenties and thirties were for a long time excluded from discussions of modernism (invisible because of their Scottishness as well as their gender, perhaps), and from critical discussions of the Scottish Renaissance (which was presented as a predominantly male movement). We are now, however, learning about the active personal and literary relationships between these women writers as well as their literary friendships with men. Nan Shepherd's and Naomi Mitchison's correspondence with Neil Gunn has already been uncovered (Hart and Pick, Donald Smith). Shepherd's encouragement of Jessie Kesson is now known and Muir showed an appreciative awareness of Morrison's work, writing of it in a less satirical spirit than she showed towards Auden, Eliot, MacDiarmid, Maurice Lindsay and other male authors in her birthday verses for Edwin:

> N. Brysson Morrison
> is a gowk if there was ever one,
> for instead of being a
> ranter and roarer
> she writes good novels
> and so the Scots ignore her. (Muir, 1951–53)

We do not yet fully know how much some of these writers were aware of earlier Scottish women writers such as Mary Brunton, Susan Ferrier or Margaret Oliphant, or how they felt about them (for we have learned from Gilbert and Gubar that women may feel ambivalent about not only their male but their female literary predecessors), though Muir, certainly, was very enthusiastic in her broadcast talk on Susan Ferrier (14 November 1954). These writers were aware of each other and of women writers beyond Scotland. Muir published her *Women: An Enquiry* (1925) with Virginia and Leonard Woolf's Hogarth Press and we now know that Kesson admired Virginia Woolf (Kesson 1994). Interesting connections are revealed, too, through assessment of reviewing work: for example, Rebecca West and Katherine Mansfield both reviewed Carswell's *Open the Door!*. Carswell, in turn, reviewed many writers of her time, both female and male.

Carswell met and corresponded with various well-known English literary figures, and spent much of her life beyond Scotland, being based for a long time in London. West, Mitchison and Muir, too, participated in the English (or 'British') as well as the specifically Scottish literary scene, and were often deeply aware of cultural developments on the Continent and further afield as well. Many of these women were highly sophisticated and wide-ranging in their reading, aware of the work of thinkers like Freud and Jung and developments in psychoanalysis and psychology, and versed in the anthropological writings of James Frazer and others, which influenced their fiction. The two post-World War Two writers both left Scotland; Kesson's long and productive career in radio drama took her to London, and Spark's whole literary career has been international; her first published story drew on her African experience, she has lived in London and New York and is now resident in Italy.

The period in which these women grew up and developed as writers was, of course, one of considerable change and conflict. Many of our writers lived through, or in the aftermath of, the First World War, which affected them, feeding into their fiction in a range of ways. Shepherd tackles the War in *The Weatherhouse*, while Rebecca West dealt with it in her first novel *The Return of the Soldier* (1918). Economic depression led to social unrest and political agitation; yet the twenties and thirties in Scotland were a time of cultural vitality, which saw the flourishing of the 'Scottish Renaissance' in literature, and a self-consciousness about identity stimulated in part by the pressure for Home Rule. Women played their own roles in political developments. Suffrage activism, as Elspeth King and Leah Leneman have demonstrated, took place in Scotland as much as in other parts of the United Kingdom; consciously taken up as a theme by Rebecca West, the fight for women's rights in the first part of the century undoubtedly affects the thinking of many writers in subtle and complex ways. Women, although partly enfranchised in 1918 and fully granted the vote in 1928, were still far from being entirely 'liberated'.

Education has long been of key significance for women writers. Some of the writers examined here were not educated beyond school level. Those who went on to higher education were often blocked in their progress; Willa Muir and Nan Shepherd, for instance, both graduated from universities and indeed became lecturers, but such women faced stark choices between careers or marriage. Women teachers who married were not permitted full-time employment, and it was not until the 1945 Education (Scotland) Act that they could marry and retain their jobs (Bird, 75). Willa Muir gave up her lecturing job after marrying Edwin; it is hardly suprising that she, like some of the other writers, dwelt with irony and some bitterness on the inequalities faced by women of her time. Education, often seen in Scottish novels as a means of 'getting on', is explored or implied as a means of escape or betterment in many of the novels discussed here, but it is also often problematised, as in *The Quarry Wood*, and the difficulties faced by the educated woman are exposed, as in Muir's own *Imagined Corners*.

Most of these writers express dissatisfaction with society as they perceived it. Some were explicitly critical. West wrote angrily about inequalities of the education question (West, 1923). Muir, like West, wrote substantial essays on feminist issues, while Mitchison, for most of her life politically active, was involved, among other campaigns, in writing pamphlets on birth control and other matters of importance to women. A writer such as Morrison, on the other hand, chooses more covert forms of protest in her fiction, which obliquely exposes the cramped and thwarted lives of women. It can be argued that all these novels raise questions about what is political. Hugh MacDiarmid, often seen as the key figure in early twentieth century Scottish literature, has set the trend for later understandings of what is 'political' in Scottish literature. Although he published poetry by some women, he was unappreciative of the novel form generally, and of women novelists in particular. He was dismissive of Violet Jacob's *Flemington* (1911) and Carswell's *Open the Door*, and was clearly ill at ease with Rebecca West's work (MacDiarmid, 1925, 1926). But all these writers can now be seen as implicitly political.

Women's writing has often been seen as 'confessional' in aspect; and while the whole field of autobiographical writing is now, rightly, being reassessed, the novelists examined here were neither representing nor in any simple sense 'reflecting' their lives in fiction, but creating fictions. Nor are they limited to any single narrative method. Carswell, Shepherd and Muir, for instance, are early experimentalists (of different kinds), working out of the cultural changes wrought by modernism, as was the early Mitchison in her own way. Although in their creation of particularised and convincingly realised worlds writers like Mitchison and West might be seen as partial realists, there are powerful mythic strains in their fiction, and elements of fantasy.

An interest in the supernatural, linked to the concern with balladry and folk culture, can be discerned in many of these novels as well. Morrison's daughters of the Manse dwell in a world haunted by the past and by ghosts both evil and benign; the north-east, the locale for the fiction of Shepherd and Kesson, is rich in folk-lore. It is the sense which they convey of the proximity of 'other worlds', their exploration of the 'liminal', that connects these novelists with earlier writers such as Margaret Oliphant (in her 'supernatural' fiction), and the poets Violet Jacob, Marion Angus and Helen Cruickshank. Scottish writers are also often deeply preoccupied with, or influenced by religion, especially Calvinism. But some show a concern with a spirituality that is not defined by religion, that may be damaged or warped by the established church, as is suggested in the work of Morrison and Muir. Such issues can be found in the work of male writers like Neil Gunn and Lewis Grassic Gibbon, but have been insufficiently recognised in the fiction of their female contemporaries, whose engagement is often subtly different.

In a range of ways, not only in terms of plot, but also of technique, these writers subvert the dominant ideologies of their times. Humour is a powerful weapon. Like earlier writers (Ferrier, Oliphant, Jacob) many of these writers employ wit and irony to expose and ridicule the structures of power that enclose women. As Willa Muir wrote in *Belonging*, 'by the time I went to England I was already alert to the comedy of my position as a woman in a patriarchally-minded country' (141); her critique of patriarchal society can also be seen in *Imagined Corners* where God is viewed by Elise as 'merely an enforcer of taboos' (185). The character of Emmy in Morrison's *The Gowk Storm* describes her father's assistant minister as 'such a preposterous man who sees everything out of proportion, particularly himself'(130). Spark in *The Prime of Miss Jean Brodie* (1961) ridicules Calvinism and the narrow Presbyterianism of Jean Brodie's fellow teachers: 'those many who had stalked past Miss Brodie in the corridors saying good morning with predestination in their smiles' (75).

Many of the works examined here are novels of development, most obviously *Open the Door!*, *The Quarry Wood* and *The White Bird Passes*, focusing as they do on the childhood and young womanhood of their protagonists. While these novels belong in a recognisable tradition, that of the bildungsroman, they differ from male versions in exploring female experience and showing, either explicitly or implicitly, the constraining effects of a patriarchal society (Abel). When they deal with family structures, those focusing on the traditional family almost inevitably represent it in critical terms; for instance the works by Carswell, Muir and Morrison. Spark presents the family unit in ironical terms in *The Ballad of Peckham Rye*. The figure of the father, whether present or absent is shown as negative or repressive in West, Carswell, Morrison and Kesson. The family in Nan Shepherd's *The Quarry Wood* contains in Geordie one of the few positive father figures; in this novel it is the mother's attitudes which are questioned. Muir's *Mrs Ritchie* is an extreme example of the mother as monster. Thus, though mother figures are often extremely important in these novels, there is no simple celebration of motherhood. The novels show alternatives to the birth mother in characters like Aunt Josephine in *The Quarry Wood*, or Elise, much more ambiguously, in *Imagined Corners*. The extended family in *The Weatherhouse* bears comparison with the community of Our Lady's Lane in *The White Bird Passes* in that both are primarily communities of women. Though neither are represented in sentimental terms, these communities seem to provide a less repressive alternative to the traditional family.

Single women in these novels often suggest alternative ways of being, from the eccentricities of Aunt Perdy in *Open the Door!* to the sturdy independence of Aunt Sally in *The Quarry Wood*. Among the more radical figures in these novels is Elise in *Imagined Corners*, who defies convention by running off with a married man, and then not marrying until later in life (to a different man). *Imagined Corners* is particularly frank in its treatment of sexual feelings, including the possibility of a lesbian relationship at the end. Of the other novelists, Mitchison is the most explicit in her exploration of sexuality, also dealing openly (and sympathetically) with same-sex love, while Kesson deals frankly with Helen Riddel's discovery of her sexual needs in *Glitter of Mica*.

Just as the idea of 'family' is interrogated, so too there is ambivalence in the representation of 'home'. 'Home' can be the literal small space of the family home, but also the familiar area of upbringing, whether rural, small-town or urban, and even the idea of Scotland itself. All these can trap, deny or suppress. While many Scottish novelists of both sexes explore contradictory feelings about 'home', in women's writing there may be further issues linked to the house as domestic space (Elphinstone) which can be confining. The actual and social structures created by human beings often represent entrapment. Joanna Bannerman in Carswell's *Open the Door* struggles with the stifling atmosphere of her family residence, dominated as it is by her father's banner, 'As for me and my house, we shall serve the Lord'(26). Yet home, especially in the larger senses of region or nation, can also be loved, as it is by Joanna. Such conflict is also explored in Shepherd's *The Quarry Wood*; and even Elise in *Imagined Corners* is drawn by memories of the home town that so constricted her, although she eventually rejects it and leaves again.

Landscape, on the other hand, both literal and metaphoric, is often presented as representative of possibilities of openness and expansion; for example in Shepherd's *The Weatherhouse*, 'the night astonished her, so huge it was. She had the sense of escaping from the lit room into light itself' (29) (Christianson, 127–9). The conventional linking of women to nature and men to culture can be limiting, but in many of these novels the natural world offers the protagonists a sense of freedom, of inspiration or of spiritual solace. This suggests the possibility of a reclamation of nature for women without necessarily limiting them to that traditional binary opposition of woman/nature and man/culture. But even landscape sometimes suggests enclosure: 'when I saw the sweep of sky joining the sea at the pale horizon, I thought of the light, waning to wax, imprisoned in the globe of the world' (*The Gowk Storm* 98). In the same novel, landscape is often shown as menacing and threatening, metaphorically suggesting the fragility of human existence.

All our writers interrogate or break down accepted conventions in a variety of ways. 'For women, the condition of patriarchy presupposes the reality of borders, even if, for women, these are often internalised borders experienced as exclusion' (Humm, 1). Maggie Humm, examining the 'significance of cultural borders' (4) discusses the ways in which women writers in the twentieth century are 'border travellers', who transgress borders and boundaries of various kinds. Such transgression, she argues, may be found especially in the work of women who are marginalised in particular ways. Many of the writers considered in this volume show strong interest in figures marginalised by society (see the work of Shepherd and Kesson, for example), and in 'borderline' kinds of experience. Willa Muir evokes the borderlands between waking and sleeping, conscious and unconscious when young Elizabeth traverses the space between land and sea, and also confronts the borders between passion and reason. Both Morrison and Shepherd appear interested in near-mystical states, although their work is still firmly rooted in the physical world, suggesting strongly the importance of human connection and community. The very conception of human identity that emerges from the work of these women writers may be subtly different from that found in writing by men in the same period; it has been argued by Patricia Waugh that women writers this century '(whether consciously feminist or not) have sought alternative conceptions of subjectivity, expressing a definition of relationship which does not make identity dependent axiomatically upon the maintenance of boundaries and distance, nor upon the subjugation of the other' (*Feminine Fictions*, 22). Waugh's perception of a concern with 'connection' may be usefully applied to the work of Scottish women writers, as may her identification, in formal aesthetic terms, of a 'breaking down of boundaries, loosening distinct outlines, merging the individual with collective, and exploring the ambiguity of identity at the interface of subject and object' (80-1).

The texts under consideration here, as a number of our essays suggest, defer 'meaning' and refuse simple readings. Through counterpointing points of view, through complex use of symbolism and metaphor, by a range of narrative strategies, they unsettle certainty in the reader. The importance of perception, of perspective, emerges as a recurring concern. These writers imply there is no single way of seeing. Yet while they are often deconstructive of dominant ideologies, some of the novels looked at here pose a challenge to the modern critic, for they are not all 'politically correct' in contemporary terms. Interests in eugenics, in race memory, in the significance of kingship and the ruling classes – these are all concerns which appear (in West, Morrison and Mitchison) and which may seem unattractive today. Furthermore the shifting meanings of the word 'feminist' make its use as a descriptive term problematic and interestingly complex; for example while it is easy to argue that Muir offers a feminist interpretation of society in *Imagined Corners*, neither Carswell nor Spark are writers whose work can necessarily be described as feminist. We have to be careful about imposing late twentieth century ideas of what feminism signifies on to these writings. In conjunction with the use of critical theory to approach these texts in new ways, we think it is essential to retain a sense of historical context.

We began with the variety of the fiction under discussion in this volume; our contributors, too, take a variety of approaches. The essays in this volume draw on a range of critical and theoretical ideas, and it is possible to see ways in which theory can be helpful in developing new ways of working with Scottish women's writing. Like most examinations of traditions in women's writing, this volume is implicitly indebted to the groundbreaking work of American 'gynocritics' like Elaine Showalter and Sandra Gilbert and Susan Gubar. The work of other theorists has also helped to open up new approaches to Scottish literature, and women's writing in particular. Several of these essays, stimulated by Hélène Cixous, focus on the ways binary oppositions might be deconstructed, and the theoretical work of Julia Kristeva and Mikhail Bakhtin also offers suggestive perspectives on the construction of social and psychic identity. An awareness of historical and material conditions underlies much of our work; yet while all these theoretical approaches enrich our reading, like Elise in Muir's *Imagined Corners*, we 'distrust any systematic interpretation of everything' (170).

Works Cited

Abel, Elizabeth et al eds.*The Voyage In: Fictions of Female Development*. Hanover, N.H.: University Press of New England, 1983
Bird, Liz 'Women and Art Education' in *Glasgow Girls* Jude Burkhauser ed. Edinburgh: Canongate, 1990, 71–9
Carswell, Catherine *Open the Door!*. 1920; Edinburgh: Canongate, 1996
Christianson, Aileen 'Imagined Corners to Debatable Land: Passable Boundaries,' *Scottish Affairs*. no.17. Autumn 1996, 120–34

Elphinstone, Margaret 'Four Pioneering Novels', *Chapman*. no. 74–5. Autumn/Winter, 1993, 23–39

Gonda, Caroline ed. *Tea and Leg-Irons: New Feminist Readings from Scotland*. London: Open Letters, 1992

Gifford, Douglas and Dorothy McMillan eds. *The History of Scottish Women's Writing*. Edinburgh: Edinburgh University Press, 1997

Gilbert, Sandra M. and Susan Gubar *No Man's Land: The Place of the Woman Writer in the Twentieth Century* 3 vols. New Haven: Yale University Press, 1988, 1989, 1994

Hart, F.R. and J.B.Pick *Neil M. Gunn: A Highland Life*. London: John Murray, 1981

Humm, Maggie *Border Traffic: Strategies of Contemporary Women Writers*. Manchester: Manchester University Press, 1991

Kesson, Jessie 'Dances with Woolf', *Scotland on Sunday*. 2 October 1994, 17

King, Elspeth *The Scottish Women's Suffrage Movement*. Glasgow: People's Palace Museum, 1978

Leneman, Leah '*A Guid Cause*' – *The Women's Suffrage Movement in Scotland*. Aberdeen: Aberdeen University Press, 1991

MacDiarmid, Hugh 'Violet Jacob', *The Scottish Educational Journal*. 17 July 1925, reprinted in *Contemporary Scottish Studies*. Edinburgh: The Scottish Educational Journal, 1976, 8–10

MacDiarmid, Hugh 'Newer Scottish Fiction (2)', *The Scottish Educational Journal*. 2 July 1926, reprinted in *Contemporary Scottish Studies*, 110-11 (with comments on Carswell)

Mansfield, Katherine 'Reviews: A Prize Novel', *Athenaeum*. 25 June 1920, 831 (review of Carswell's *Open the Door!*)

Muir, Willa *Imagined Corners*. 1931; Edinburgh: Canongate, 1996

Muir, Willa *Belonging: A Memoir*. London: Hogarth, 1968

Muir, Willa 'Ephemeridae' [1951 or 1952] and 'Ephemeridae' (2)', 1953. National Library of Scotland: Edwin and Willa Muir papers, MS 19703. 39–54

Muir, Willa 'Susan Ferrier' (typescript). St Andrews University: Willa Muir papers, MS deposit 9.2, 14 Nov. 1954

Shepherd, Nan *The Living Mountain*. 1977; Edinburgh: Canongate, 1996

Showalter, Elaine *A Literature of Their Own: British Women Novelists from Bronte to Lessing*. London: Virago, 1977

Smith, Donald 'Naomi Mitchison and Neil Gunn: A Highland Friendship', *Cencrastus*. no.13. Summer 1983, 17-20

Waugh, Patricia *Feminine Fictions: Revisiting the Postmodern*. London: Routledge, 1989

West, Rebecca 'Six Point Group Supplement Point No.3. Equality for Men and Women Teachers', *Time and Tide*. 9 Feb.1923, reprinted in *Time and Tide Wait for No Man*, Dale Spender ed. London: Pandora Press, 1984, 54-7

West, Rebecca 'Notes on Novels', *New Statesman*. 5 June 1920, 253–4 (review of Carswell's *Open the Door!*)

Whyte, Christopher ed. *Gendering the Nation: Studies in Modern Scottish Literature*. Edinburgh: Edinburgh University Press, 1995

Catherine Carswell (1879–1946)

Born Catherine Roxburgh Macfarlane in Glasgow in 1879, the second of four children of the deeply religious ('wee Free') George and Mary Anne Macfarlane, this writer studied music in Frankfurt, and English at Glasgow University, gaining the attention of Professor Walter Raleigh (though women could not graduate). She married Herbert Jackson in 1904, but his mental illness soon became apparent, and the marriage was annulled in 1908. Their daughter Diana was born in 1905. Catherine, who had been living in the south of England, returned to Glasgow and began her journalistic career as a drama critic and book reviewer for the *Glasgow Herald*. After her mother's death in 1912, Catherine moved to London, where Diana died in 1913. Catherine lost her *Glasgow Herald* job when she reviewed her friend D.H.Lawrence's *The Rainbow* in 1915. After a long affair with married painter Maurice Greiffenhagen, she married Donald Carswell in 1915; he was a scholarly man, who shared Catherine's literary interests, but the couple struggled to make a living by their writing. Their son John wrote introductions to Carswell's two novels *Open the Door!* (1920) and *The Camomile* (1922) and her autobiographical *Lying Awake* (1950) which includes some of her correspondence. Catherine Carswell also wrote biographies: her lively, contentious *The Life of Robert Burns* of 1930 (reissued by Canongate), a life of D.H.Lawrence, *The Savage Pilgrimage* (also considered controversial in its time), and *The Tranquil Heart*, a biography of fourteenth-century Italian writer Giovanni Boccaccio (1937). Catherine Carswell died in 1946.

C.A.

'Behold I make all things new': Catherine Carswell and the Visual Arts

Carol Anderson

Catherine Carswell's *Open the Door!*, started around 1911 though not published until 1920, traces the childhood and young womanhood of Joanna Bannerman. Joanna attends the Glasgow School of Art and works as a designer; she frequents an 'artistic' circle, has a long love affair with a painter, Louis Pender, and a friendship with the Master of Design at the Art School. Eventually Joanna earns a living in London.

Open the Door! is not really a Künstlerroman like Carswell's second novel, *The Camomile*, which explores the development of Ellen Carstairs from musician to committed writer. Joanna in *Open the Door!* is sensitive and creative, but described as limited in talent; like her sister Georgie, she may 'turn for help to the fine arts', but 'neither was greatly gifted' (47). The extent of her genius is suggested by the fact that 'at school she generally carried off a second prize for drawing' (50). By the end of the novel, unlike Joyce's Stephen Dedalus, Joanna still has no aspirations to be a great artist.

Nevertheless, the novel was written at a time when the relationship between literature, painting and music was often close; in her essay 'Walter Sickert', Virginia Woolf wrote that 'though they must part in the end, painting and writing have much to tell each other: they have much in common. The novelist, after all, wants to make us see' (1925; 1966, 241). *Open the Door!*, for all the modesty of its heroine's artistic ambitions, is both thematically and formally involved with all the visual arts, particularly those of Scotland.

Carswell had personal contact with the visual arts which informed and inspired her work. She remembers 'with details recorded as if by a Dutch painter of interiors' (1997, 93) her first visit to the family of Uncle Frank, 'a Calabrian and a painter' (1997, 94), who painted the young Catherine. Carswell grew up in Garnethill, where the Glasgow School of Art was built according to Mackintosh's plans (1897–9, 1907–9), and was attended by one of her closest school-friends (1997, 119), Phyllis Clay, later a sculptor (John Carswell, 1996, xiii). Catherine herself took evening classes there ,[1] and had a long and passionate affair with the painter Maurice Greiffenhagen, from 1906 the director of the Life Class (John Carswell,1996, viii), whose work was admired by Carswell's friend, D.H. Lawrence. Lawrence read *Open the Door!* before publication, as Carswell read *Women in Love*. She was critical of Lawrence's 'arty' characters in the latter (1932, 38), but her novel engages with some of the same concerns. Marianna Torgovnick, discussing modern novels which 'use the visual arts', expresses their degrees of involvement in terms of the visual image of a 'continuum', at one end of which are the 'decorative', or slighter uses of the visual arts, the deeper and more significant uses being ideological and interpretive. *Open the Door!*, permeated with the visual, not only through its concern with artists but through its narrative methods, is simultaneously decorative and 'ideological'.

Some recent criticism has found the novel frustrating. Although in Joanna we have 'a heroine who could be remarkably interesting', being in some ways daring and independent, Smith comments: 'we get no real idea of the kind of work she does, we get little notion of Joanna herself outside the ebb and flow of her emotions for whichever man is her love of the moment' (1995, 28); she also identifies a conservative concern with nature in the novel (1995, 29–30), whose conclusion has been particularly criticised. Pam Morris remarks that although *Open the Door!* initially delineates a 'precise historical moment and social group in Glasgow at the beginning of the century', it focuses increasingly on the private and individual, especially the sexual, thereby being 'depoliticised' (1993, 142–3). These critical accounts make useful points, but convey little sense of the novel's rich texture, which allows plural readings. Threads woven in its fabric, through an interest in the visual, modify the idea of the novel as narrow in its concerns, as simply reactionary, or 'depoliticised'. There is engagement in *Open the Door!* with questions about the role of art and its relationship to nature and to life, for instance; and while the influence of Lawrence has often, rightly, been acknowledged, the novel's broad concern with, and assertion of, cultural identity, may also be read in the context of Carswell's own Scottish artistic environment. Finally, although this is not an overtly 'political' text, it is possible to construct feminist readings even of its conclusion.

Seeing the work in its historical context enables appreciation of both its social and aesthetic concerns, which straddle late nineteenth and early twentieth-century traditions. Juley Bannerman's aims for her daughters are that they should be able to support themselves if they do not marry or turn missionary; it is to this 'practical end' that Joanna 'was allowed to forsake her High School for the School of Art when she was barely seventeen' (50). Joanna's 'ambition was to earn her own living' (159). The novel is set at a time when women were being actively encouraged in the Applied Arts at Glasgow School of Art under its innovative Director, Fra Newbery (appointed 1885). Women teaching there, like Jessie Newbery, redefined such traditionally feminine areas as embroidery. Through craft and design activities, women had a chance to find some personal fulfilment and earn a living (Walker, 169).

Several characters in the novel, notably Joanna herself, design and make things decorated with motifs drawn from nature, as in the Arts and Crafts, and specifically Glasgow manner; Jessie Newbery, in reality, designed and made dresses, often favouring the colour green and incorporating botanical motifs (Arthur, 147). Joanna, in the novel, designs and wears a dress she has made at the School of Art: 'her spreading apple-green skirt crinkled as petals that are folded in a poppy bud' (56). Joanna's brother Sholto, though unassociated with the Art School, fashions small items of furniture 'and afterwards poker-worked them' (81), making her a present of a toilet set 'all with the same lily-of- the-valley design' (106). Joanna works commercially, being invited to submit designs for a leading drapery firm (197), and makes as a gift a box with a 'bright, impossible bird on the lid' (328). Although women's working lives are not extensively explored in the novel, the 'holistic' approach (Walker, 167) of this feminine-accented milieu is evoked: functional objects are made beautiful with organic designs, art is linked to nature, and is part of everyday life, not something 'high' or 'apart'. A whole aesthetic is implied which pervades the novel.

This highly-wrought fiction makes metaphorical reference to the Applied Arts: in the 'arch' of the sky 'hung the pale waxing moon like a beaker of fretted silver' (100); the 'voice' of dripping water is 'frail as filigree' (388); Joanna hears sounds distinctly 'as an embroidress might separate a skein of silken threads' (402). Other 'decorative' passages, too, appear 'influenced by the visual arts and suggest a particular movement or an actual work' (Torgovnick, 14). There are echoes of the contemporary, design-led interest in Japanese art: [2] the stone pines with 'their black tufts and tassels showing in Japanese detail against the sky' (65), and the account of Joanna's face, like Aunt Perdy's, as having 'a faintly Japanese suggestion, a flatness of structure' (88). In another scene on a bridge Joanna gazes at the city: 'tier upon tier of flats full of windows seemed in the darkness to be a dense forest screen hung unevenly with barred, many coloured lanterns' (63). This visually complex passage describes the man-made world in terms of an artfully-arranged natural world, as when Joanna sits in the hall of the new family home, and 'in the dusk of the spring evening the round stone pillars on either side of her might have been tree-trunks' (261).

The interest in design and the yoking of art and nature echo the work of Margaret and Frances Macdonald, Charles Rennie Mackintosh and other Glasgow artists. Carswell probably absorbed some of the same influences as them (literary, cultural, artistic), and 'would have been familiar with Mackintosh's work' (Kinchin, 54–5), especially since even after his departure from Glasgow in 1914, Mackintosh communicated with Carswell's lover, Greiffenhagen (Neat, 174). The narrative's visual images paralleling or invoking 'Glasgow Style' provide much of its power and beauty; they cumulatively create a distinctive vision stressing interconnectedness and communality, and a context, too, within which aesthetic questions can be raised and tested. The decorative arts have often been seen as 'lesser' than so-called 'high art', but this novel implicitly calls such hierarchy into question and also 'the view of the artist as a separated, isolated genius' (DuPlessis, 104; see also Pilditch, 60–1). This is particularly seen when two of Joanna's lovers are considered; not merely sexual figures but creators of different kinds, they embody an artistic debate within the novel's framework.

For D. H. Lawrence, 'an ideological use of the visual arts embodies major themes of the fiction' (Torgovnick, 19). Lawrence's critical fascination with the Futurists influenced the writing of *Women in Love*. Futurist ideology, which was theorised by an Italian, Filippo Marinetti, rejected tradition, was 'dedicated to the celebration of new technologies and the excitement of an accelerated pace of life and change' (Stevenson, 9), and seen by D.H. Lawrence as representing 'the purely male or intellectual or scientific line' (Lawrence,181), is suggested in Carswell's novel by the figure of Joanna's aggressively masculine Italian lover, Mario Rasponi. Mario 'was energy itself; but energy pent, not radiant. His body was like a coiled spring of steel'(93); his mother was the 'daughter of a professor of mechanics at Turin'(115), and what interests him most is machinery (99). Mario has been attempting to build a machine that can fly, but in a novel where birds suggest spirituality, his mechanical, purely materialist attempts are doomed. This arrogant, self-willed individualist dies travelling 'at great speed' on his 'auto-velocipede', driving on the 'wrong side of the road' (134). The novel suggests his is not the way forward.

There are also scenes suggesting opposition between his approach, and the holistic traditions of Joanna's culture. Mario appreciates the beauty of the wine-glasses which Joanna buys from a second-hand shop, 'set exquisitely on their octagonal stems, they were like the calyxes of water–lilies' (68). Inscribed with a floral design, 'the lovely wine-glasses that were like river water full of the shimmer of wavelets and criss-cross reeds' (104), echo both the Arts and Crafts concern with nature, and images in Carswell's novel on objects, in metaphors (Joanna as flower, 273), and in symbolism (water, the pond). It is therefore significant that the jealous Mario shatters the glasses, having identified them as probably Irish (104), an allusion to the Celtic Art Revival, stimulated by Irish nationalism, and promoted in Scotland notably by Patrick Geddes in his journal *The Evergreen* (1895–7), 'A Northern Seasonal'. Celtic art influenced the great Glasgow designers, feeding into the elongated forms typical of 'Glasgow Style' (Burkhauser, 96–7); in the novel, in a racial theme which may seem problematic today but was common at the time, Joanna's Celtic 'roots' are suggested in the unconvincing but important dancing scene, where we learn that her forebears included a Stirlingshire farmer's daughter and a Welsh soldier (169).

Specificity of culture is important in a novel which establishes a strong sense of place. Joanna's discontent with Glasgow is implied in a city scene of river and willows (65). The willow is meaningful here, for the name of Glasgow's Sauchiehall Street, of Celtic origin, derives from the Gaelic for willow, and the Willow Tea Room, designed and decorated by Mackintosh and Macdonald with a gesso panel based on D. G. Rossetti's poem 'O Ye That Walk in Willow-wood', was opened there in 1903. When Mario talks about the olive tree of his native Italy, Joanna identifies the willow as like a 'cage' (101). Yet despite dreams of escape, she rebukes Mario for calling her English (101). Joanna 'stared persistently at the willow. "Look at me," he repeated. "Why should I look at you," she opposed him with low-voiced obstinacy, "if I want to go on looking at the tree?"' (102). This symbolic moment has resonances throughout the novel, which repeatedly returns Joanna to Scotland and its arts, appearing to endorse them in the face of alternatives.

Louis Pender, another kind of creator, is the great love of Joanna's life for much of the novel, and the affair is powerfully evoked. However, almost from the first, his art suggests his limitations: 'Could it be possible that he was only a fan painter?' (191). Louis is a society man with small-scale ambitions. No serious artistic experimenter – 'he had to work in fetters' (193) – he enjoys extra-marital love, but in life, as in art, he will not leave those 'fetters' of convention; indeed, he is open about his need of them (227), refusing to give Joanna his paintings as his wife would not like it (281–2).

Louis lacks cultural identity, too. He has no positive memories of his own childhood, insensitively recoiling from the scenes of Joanna's early life (218); like Mario, Louis is largely indifferent to Glasgow, despising the architecture of the Art Gallery (built 1901) and the building materials of the city (220–1). His art, ominously, has a 'beauty full of farewells' (192); Louis, 'Joanna's fascinating symbol for the greatly coveted world of mammon' (268) belongs to the past, in Carl Nilsson's terms, 'a man that's dead as dead'(288).

These creators represent alternative ways of seeing, of creating, of *living*, their art, in a novel which stresses interconnectedness, shown as inextricable from lifestyle and values. The novel's own techniques and procedures, like those of Glasgow art of the time, suggest a very different way of viewing the world from the mechanical (Mario), or the social and conventional (Pender). Glasgow around the turn of the century was 'one of the European centres of Ruskinian thought and consciously symbolist art' (Neat, 20). Glasgow artists, like other contemporaries, 'abstracted elements of the real world to illustrate allegorical and literary themes of life and death, decay and renewal, night and day, good and evil, as well as the world of dreams and the imagination' (Robertson, 298). This same complex relationship between dreams and life is evoked symbolically in *Open the Door!* in some of its most intensely visual passages: Joanna's dream of her father seen through the stained-glass door (27–8), and the later image of Louis, like her father, satyr-like, also seen through glass (265). Like Mackintosh's enigmatic 'Harvest Moon' of 1894, this fiction 'may well deal with the opposing themes of chastity and abandon, of Christianity and paganism' (Robertson, 300). Joanna's spiritual quest is suggested through colours: pearly shades (59, 64–5), silver and blue, yet there is eroticism too. Joanna and Bob cling together on a staircase 'in the dark–blue middle air' (61); in Italy, scene of Joanna's sexual education, the sky 'palpitated from blue to violet, from violet to a still deeper blue' (122).

Many of the novel's symbols and motifs – water, seeds, birds – are similar to those found in works like Frances Macdonald's 'A Pond' (1894) or Margaret Macdonald's 'The Path of Life' (1894). Birds, so important a symbol in this novel, fly across the moon in the background of Frances Macdonald's 'Ill Omen' (1893) (used by Virago for the cover of their edition of the novel). A disturbing description in the novel of the 'strangely long' child Edvina Moon, with her 'piteous mouth', echoes the elongated figures of the 'Spook School', [3] 'the close-cropped skull' with 'its sharp temples so transparent and blue-veined' (296) sounding like the strange, androgynous figures found in the Macdonalds' work: 'the dilated nostrils, fragile as porcelain, had no recollection of the pain by which they had been purged into what they were. Miss Moon was like some sea-shell, delicately empty, cast high upon the beach, which it has taken the whole cruel ocean to blow into shape, to flute and carve and lave to a foam-like whiteness' (297). The paradoxical existence of death in life is suggested visually and symbolically. The novel, illustrating both binary oppositions and their breakdown, prompts particular comparisons with Frances Macdonald, whose work, Burkhauser (131) suggests, may be read fruitfully in the light of Hélène Cixous' work. Cixous argues that in the system of 'dual, hierarchical oppositions' (1986, 64) which dominates western thought, female is generally linked with passivity, male with activity. Cixous exposes these and other binary oppositions which generally uphold masculine power, and, deconstructing them, suggests that women cannot be contained within, or described by, such a limiting system. Cixous' own work implies the 'plurality'of femininity, and resists the idea of unitary meaning. It may be argued in the light of such ideas that the most powerful symbolic moments in Carswell's work suggest no single fixed meaning.

As in *Women in Love* this novel's 'pictorial images allow themes and issues to resonate in characters' and readers' minds without the kind of explicit verbalizing that might flatten the novel' (Torgovnick, 212). But there is also 'explicit verbalising'. In an early pictorial scene in *Open the Door!* Joanna, as a child on a train crossing a bridge over the River Clyde, looks out on a scene vividly described, with allusions to colour, light and movement reminiscent of Impressionist painting, (see Carswell, 1997, 119), and an emphasis on the pattern and framing so important to the Glasgow designers, thus introducing Joanna's symbolic way of seeing: 'This picture, cut into sections and made brilliant by the interposing trellis of black metal, appealed not so much to the little girl's untrained eye, as symbolically through her eye to her heart which leapt in reponse' (7).

Randall Stevenson points to an aspect of some modernist fiction, 'a kind of self-reflexiveness in which texts talk about their own methods, or artists discuss or demonstrate problems and priorities that also figure in the construction of the novel in which they appear' (165). Joanna's symbolic vision forms a vital and self-conscious part of the novel's own technique: 'Birds had always played a memorable part in her dreams, persisting there like a symbol' (141). Joanna frequently broods on meanings; when her (symbolically named) brother Linnet leaves, 'Like a key the master symbol of her life heretofore was put into her hand: Ev'nas a bird/Out of the fowler's snare/Escapes away/So is our soul set free! '(354). Carswell may be uncertain of her audience's understanding (Elphinstone, 24), but the deliberate underlining of symbols is functional, drawing attention to a particular way of seeing and expressing. Dialogues between Joanna and Lawrence Urquhart,

Carl Nilsson's metaphorically-expressed interpretation of their relationship (the seed and the clod), and Lawrence Urquhart's caveat ' Images,though, are apt to be misleading '(369) are obviously related to the novel's own strategies, arguably contributing to its examination of art forms and their relationship to life.

This novel encourages the reader to 'see', and to think about 'ways of seeing', both through its characters and techniques, and although its last scenes have been criticised (Smith 29, Morris 143, Elphinstone 27), they exemplify its consistent self-conscious concern with 'vision' (in several senses). Towards the end, Joanna, who had once kissed an old blind woman (29–30) thinks of humanity as 'a flock of blind things, each one trusting implicitly, as she had done, in the corporate blindness of all the other blind ones.' (363). By the end it seems that Joanna may be learning truly to 'see': she realises that 'the desire of sacrifice and the desire of pride', between which she had been torn, were falsely opposed, for 'both had been needed' (420); now, 'that period of her life – conscious and striving, but blind – was past' (420). Through a kind of wise passivity, it implies, she achieves 'true' vision or insight; yet here again binary oppositions are challenged, for Joanna is not entirely passive. In the final scene stressing her new, true 'seeing' (both visual and spiritual) of Lawrence Urqhuart, there is an interesting reversal of previous patterns in Joanna's relationships. As a student, in her hand-made dress, Joanna was concerned with self-presentation, willing to be an object. Mario saw her in terms of Italian art, comparing her to a work 'by a painter of the Venetian school' (94); Louis saw her as a Gothic Madonna (219), the potential destructiveness of his gaze apparent: 'Joanna could feel the unsheathed boldness of his eyes like weapons' (185). At Joanna's reunion with Lawrence, she is actively looking, not being viewed. The final scene is again represented in visual terms, like a camera filming: 'Away on the moor a jerkily moving object caught the sunlight. It was the bare, black head of a man . . .' (424). Significantly, Joanna sees Lawrence before he sees her: 'He had not seen her. He did not know. He was not even looking for her!' (424)

The ending emphasises romantic over artistic fulfilment; 'she herself would never be able to see with the painter's eye' (415); however, Joanna makes no such stark choice as Trissie Moon, once 'a promising art student' (316), had done. Her independence is achieved before romance is granted, the novel thus rejecting 'the completely binary alternatives of the nineteenth-century texts – either domestic life or artistic life' (DuPlessis, 104). And although Lawrence Urquhart, with his dominant mother and his neuralgia (366), makes an awkward lover, this relationship is not reducible to sex or conventional romance: 'the dependence of Joanna and Lawrence . . . is equal and mutual, and the perfect circle is defined as love, not sex' (Pilditch, 64). This union may not simply be Lawrentian; it reflects ideals current among Glasgow artists at this time (Kinchin, 60–1). 'The new man' and the 'new woman' are creating themselves, and a new *kind* of relationship: 'Nor did any future as yet exist for them. They were in the beginning of their new creation' (428).

Of course, Lawrence is also – perhaps above all – a symbolic figure and his schematic role (his ability at dancing, his eyes like 'peaty pools' (371) representing the 'pull' of 'home') accounts in part for his unsatisfactoriness as a character. That Joanna's final insight takes place at 'the very spot where she found her essential self in childhood' (Smith, 29) may also seem too 'tidy', and a traditionally limiting restoration of woman to nature. However, Joanna's return north is not just to nature, but to Scotland, and to a 'real place, as well as her home of dreams' (30), 'a real place after all' (415) described in detail, with a history and meaning for her. The pond at Duntarvie, that 'mysterious water' with its 'legend of the neighbour-hood' (31) is open to multiple reading, evoking the subconscious, but also overlaying culture in the form of story, on the 'natural' landscape.

It is important, too, in the novel's summation of its artistic themes, that Carl Nilsson, the 'middle aged Swedish artist' (162), who teaches Design at the Art School, reappears here. Refusing participation in Mrs Lovatt's *salon* and the purely social and superficial aspects of the Glasgow art scene, Carl's breadth of vision is implied early on through his response to Phemie's singing, and his opening of Joanna's mind to a 'lower' social group whose 'streams of being flowed bright and uncontaminated from Glasgow's central pulse. And they knew it. They were more at home in Paris than in Edinburgh' (168–9). Nilsson is broadly European, introducing Lawrence to other artists ('the half-mad Irish sculptor, Conolly' at Bruges, 236) and the life of the continent; he is Northern (as opposed to the Southern Mario), a hint at Patrick Geddes' ideal, underlying the Glasgow designers' work, too, that Scotland might 'again become, like Norway, one of the European Powers of Culture and share in that wider culture-movement which knows neither nationality nor race' (Boardman, 150).[4] Carl Nilsson, the North European cosmopolitan artist, Joanna's critic, and 'interpreter', finally unites her with Lawrence, the Scottish Folklorist. The novel, with its ethos of interconnectedness, suggests that in the union of art and nature, the European and the locally Scottish, Joanna finds harmony in her self.

This may be problematic for modern critics, whose post-structural notions of identity stress the impossibility of 'harmony'. It is frustrating, too, from a certain perspective, that Joanna's striving is pre-eminently for the 'art of life', while the figure of the male artist as mentor is privileged; Carswell here, as in *The Camomile*, is fascinated by masculine authority, and like many women writers of her time, seems uncertain and ambivalent about women's creative power. Yet the novel, in oblique ways, does suggest the power of 'the feminine'; it is Joanna's female affiliations (Aunt Georgina, 405–7) who orchestrate her return to Duntarvie, the place 'owed . . . to their mother' (30), and in the last lines, at Joanna's command 'See! The moon!', the lovers (and reader) contemplate the symbol not only of romance (Pilditch, 66) but of femininity. Carswell's novel is a large one – she is no fan-painter – and in some ways offers a challenge to contemporary orthodoxy, both social and artistic. 'Behold, I make all things new' declares the defiant epigraph to Book 3. The ending to this vividly sensous 'Scotto-Continental'[5] novel, in the context of its time and place, has a certain bold and visionary optimism.

Notes

1. I am grateful to Dr Jan Pilditch for drawing this to my attention.
2. On Japonism in Glasgow art, see Burkhauser, 97.
3. This was the name given to the work of Herbert MacNair, Charles Rennie Mackintosh, and Frances and Margaret Macdonald, when they exhibited together in 1894. See Burkhauser, 85.
4. On Patrick Geddes' influence on the Glasgow artists, see Kinchin, 32, 57, 60–1, and Burkhauser 97.
5. The term was used by H.F. Jennings in 1902 of Glasgow art. See Kinchin, 40.

Works Cited

Arthur, Liz 'Jessie Newbery' in *Glasgow Girls: Women in Art and Design 1880–1920* Jude Burkhauser ed. Edinburgh: Canongate, 1990, 147–51
Boardman, Philip *The Worlds of Patrick Geddes: Biologist, Town planner, Re-educator, Peace-warrior*. London: Routledge and Kegan Paul, 1978
Burkhauser, Jude 'The Glasgow Style' in Burkhauser ed. Edinburgh: Canongate, 1990, 81–106

Carswell, Catherine *Open the Door!*. 1920; London: Virago, 1986; Edinburgh: Canongate, 1996. With an introduction by John Carswell

Carswell, Catherine *The Savage Pilgrimage*. London: Chatto and Windus, 1932; Cambridge: Cambridge University Press, 1981

Carswell, Catherine *Lying Awake: An Unfinished Autobiography and Other Posthumous Papers*. 1950; Edinburgh: Canongate, 1997. With an introduction by John Carswell

Cixous, Hélène and Catherine Clément *The Newly Born Woman*. Betsy Wing trans. 1975; Manchester: Manchester University Press, 1986

DuPlessis, Rachel Blau *Writing Beyond the Ending: Narrative Strategies of Twentieth-Century Women Writers*. Bloomington: Indiana University Press, 1985

Elphinstone, Margaret 'Four Pioneering Novels', *Chapman*. vol. 74–5. Autumn/Winter 1993, 23–39

Kaplan, Wendy ed. *Charles Rennie Mackintosh*. New York, London, Paris: Glasgow Museums/Abbeville Press, 1996

Kinchin, Juliet 'Mackintosh and the City', in Kaplan ed., 31–63

Lawrence, D.H. *The Letters of D.H. Lawrence*. James Boulton et al eds. Cambridge: Cambridge University Press, 1979–93, vol. 2 [1981]

Morris, Pam *Literature and Feminism*. Oxford: Blackwell, 1993

Neat, Timothy *Part Seen, Part Imagined: Meaning and Symbolism in the Work of Charles Rennie Macintosh and Margaret Macdonald*. Edinburgh: Canongate, 1994

Pilditch, Jan 'Opening the Door on Catherine Carswell', *Scotlands*. 2, 1994, 53–65

Robertson, Pamela 'The Making of a Painter' in Kaplan, 291–318

Smith, Alison 'And Woman Created Woman' in *Gendering the Nation*. Christopher Whyte ed. Edinburgh: Edinburgh University Press, 1995, 25–47

Stevenson, Randall *Modernist Fiction*. Hemel Hempstead: Harvester Wheatsheaf, 1992

Torgovnick, Marianna *The Visual Arts, Pictorialism and the Novel: James, Lawrence and Woolf*. Princeton: Princeton University Press, 1985

Walker, Lynne 'The Arts and Crafts Alternative', in *A View From the Interior: Women and Design*. Judy Attfield and Pat Kirkham eds. London: Virago, 1989; new edition 1995, 165–73

Woolf, Virginia ' Walter Sickert' in *Collected Essays*. vol. 2. 1925; London: Hogarth Press, 1966, 233–44

Rebecca West (1892–1983)

Rebecca West was born Cicily Isabel Fairfield in London, in 1892. Her mother, Isabella Mackenzie was a Scot from Edinburgh, who met and married the Anglo-Irish Charles Fairfield in Australia; he left his family when Rebecca was young, and she and her two sisters were raised by their mother in Edinburgh, where they were educated, between 1901 and 1910. The young writer, who adopted the name Rebecca West from the feminist heroine of Ibsen's play *Rosmerholm*, was a suffragette activist in Edinburgh; when she moved to London, hoping to become an actress, she turned instead to journalism, writing for *The Freewoman, Time and Tide* and other feminist publications. Rebecca West wrote prolifically throughout her long life, publishing in a wide range of genres: novels, essays, biographies and travel writing. Her first novel, *The Return of the Soldier*, appeared in 1918, but perhaps her best known is *The Fountain Overflows* (1957). Her *Black Lamb and Grey Falcon* (1941), about Yugoslavia, has attracted some attention in recent times. Her long-standing relationship with H.G.Wells (who was married) led to the birth of her only son Anthony in 1914. She married a banker, Henry Maxwell Andrews, in 1930. Created a Dame Commander of the British Empire in 1959, she died in 1983.

C.A.

Feminine Space, Feminine Sentence: Rebecca West's *The Judge*

Carol Anderson

Rebecca West, usually thought of as an English writer, dwells at length in her *Family Memories* on what she calls 'the rich textures of my mother's ancestry as manufactured by the Scottish tradition' (17). Rebecca West is in no simple sense 'a Scottish writer', but her involvement with Scottish culture shaped her fiction thematically and formally. Edinburgh is the setting for the first half of *The Judge*, which is dedicated to 'the memory of my mother'. The novel's young Scottish protagonist Ellen Melville falls in love with an Englishman, Richard Yaverland, and in the work's second half moves with him to his mother's home in the Essex marshes, where Marion Yaverland's history dominates both Ellen's life and the narrative.

The Judge engages with the nature and importance of cultural tradition, and although it may be accused of trading in stereotypes – Ellen is red-headed, and the attempts to render Scots speech are unconvincing – it contains sharp observation of 'two clashing cultures' (Ray, 300). The cultural differences between Ellen and her English lover are shown fuelling a mutual attraction to 'otherness', and the relationship's inequalities are related to national identity and gender. Dialogues and shifting point of view present the characters' perspectives on each others' cultures (33–4, 37, 88–9); through Ellen the novel gives voice to a Scottish perspective (97–8), but through Richard also offers acerbic comment on the clichés of Scottish culture. The Melvilles' home, for instance, is seen through his eyes, decorated with 'big steel engravings of Highland cattle enjoying domestic life under adverse climatic conditions, and Queen Victoria giving religion a leg up by signing things in the presence of bishops' (77). The Scottish lawyer, Mactavish James, with his role-playing (147) and sentimentality (151), is seen by Richard as false and theatrical (166).

Questions of Scottish identity are ironically raised. Mactavish James, looking at Ellen breathes ' "Well, well!" – that greeting by which Scot links himself to Scot in a mutual consciousness of a prudent despondency about life' (14). Later, '[h]e pondered, with a Scotch sort of enjoyment, on the frustration of youth's hopes and the progress of mortality in himself' (130). The narrator frequently identifies Scottish 'characteristics': it is 'the note of Edinburgh, of all lowland Scotland, to rise out of ordinary life to a more than ordinary magnificence, and then to qualify that magnificence by some cynical allusion to ordinary life' (96). Such characteristics seem to be demonstrated in Ellen and arguably in the novel itself, which is both realist and melodramatic, ironic and mythic.

Several critics see something Scottish in the non-realist aspects of West's other fiction. *Harriet Hume* can be viewed as a 'Calvinist fantasy' (Marcus, 147) whose form 'has some affinity with that of R. L. Stevenson and J. M. Barrie' (Glendinning, 1980, i-ii). The novelist who took her pen-name from Ibsen also had Scottish literary fathers; the setting of *The Judge*, 'the office of Mr. Mactavish James, Writer to the Signet' (9) implicitly invokes both Scott and Stevenson, the latter being explicitly mentioned. Ellen is entranced by Richard Yaverland because he has property in Rio de Janeiro: 'it's like being related to someone in 'Treasure Island' (20). The novel's opening, considered by Ann Norton (300) to echo *Macbeth* and *Ivanhoe* also recalls Stevenson's *Edinburgh: Picturesque Notes* (the city is characterised by both West and Stevenson as 'theatrical'). Its plot as originally conceived (Glendinning, 1988, 81) contains elements reminiscent of the plans for *Weir of Hermiston* (Stevenson, Appendix A), and Richard Yaverland's vision of Ellen (32–3) recalls the scene in the church at Hermiston, when Archie gazes at young Kirsty Elliott (Chapter VI).

The novel is playfully sceptical of the status accorded Scottish cultural figures. When Richard Yaverland visits the Melvilles, he notices 'the engravings, which for the most part represented Robert Burns as the Scotch like to picture their national poet, with hair sleek and slightly waved like the coat of a retriever hanging round a face oval and blank and sweet like a tea-biscuit' (81), while Ellen declares with youthful arrogance 'I think nothing of the man. His intellectual content was miserably small' (81). For Ellen, rebelling against a male-dominated Scotland, a female figure, Mary Queen of Scots, is the only living presence in the city: 'Nobody of a like intensity had lived here since. The Covenanters, the Jacobites, Sir Walter Scott and his fellows, had dropped nothing in the pool that could break the ripples started by that stone, that precious stone, flung there from France so long ago' (16–7). Apart from Stevenson, Ellen has scant regard for the masculine traditions of Scotland, attacking her employer Mactavish James's hypocrisy: 'Why are you not more respectful to the Suffragettes? You're polite enough to the Covenanters, and yet they fought and killed people, while we haven't killed even a policeman . . . If you don't admire us you shouldn't admire the Convenanters' (143).

Hugh MacDiarmid acknowledged the novel, writing in 1926 that '*The Judge* remains – unfortunately – the best *Scottish* novel of recent years'(109). Given West's implicit attacks on patriarchal Scotland, however, it is perhaps not surprising that MacDiarmid's longer 'review' of the book, in the form of a playful dialogue between two male voices, one Scots, the other English–speaking, expresses a range of objections to her work related to language, the inadequacy of the novel form, and above all to gender. The Scots-speaking persona criticises West's attempt to represent Edinburgh in fiction: 'I'm no blamin' Miss West – but ye canna play Beethoven on an Almanie whistle! It tak's an almark like Joyce tae write aboot Edinburgh. The lassie never gets amidward. She canna be fashed wi' a' its amplefeysts – she hesna' got the necessary *animosity* . . . . It'll tak a *man* tae write aboot Edinburgh, as it sud be written aboot, an' he'll need the Doric tae get the fu' aifer . . . The verra last thing Scottish literature needs is *lady-fying*' *(MacDiarmid, 1922, 279–82)*.

Yet although MacDiarmid refused to acknowledge it, this novel is political; indeed, 'one must almost assume that the very choice of women's issues draws this attack' by the Scottish poet (Gish, 277). *The Judge* explores both public and private 'justice', probing the ideology of the time, especially as it related to women. In the novel Ellen attends suffragette meetings and demands recognition of women's legal and political rights by selling *Votes for Women* in Princes Street. The injustice of her powerlessness is underlined by her employment in a legal office, and the fact that Philip James, her employer's son, is to enter politics (23) despite his lack of idealism and his morally questionable character (42). West was deeply critical of Scottish society in *Family Memories*: 'The interests of the fathers and the sons were always considered before the interests of the mothers and the daughters, and while it is true that a woman alone is in any society as handicapped as if she had some slight deformity, it was more so in Scotland' (36). Such a perception underlies *The Judge*, which engages with dominant social ideas about women extending beyond Scotland. These ideas

permeated the legal, political and social institutions and practices that perpetuated them, and they were effective at several different levels of legal prescription, institutional discrimination and social decorum. (By *law* certain possibilities were closed to women, by precedent certain activities excluded them, by custom certain activities were not lady-like.) 'We are not governed by armies and police, we are governed by ideas,' as Mona Caird wrote in 1892 (Tickner, xi).

Among those governing ideas was the notion of separate spheres. In the nineteenth century the 'public world of work, politics, and city life...despite the presence of some women in certain contained areas of it, was a masculine domain' (Wolff, 34–5). Even into the early twentieth century, middle-class women and the idea of 'femininity' itself were still associated with the 'private' and domestic. West challenges the separate spheres by 'rejecting domestic space' in *Harriet Hume* (Marcus, 136), and in *The Judge* portraying a young, lower-middle-class woman in the 'masculine' domain of work. Yet she also shows the difficulties faced by women entering the public domain.

The Judge explores women's relationship to space, both literal and meta-phorical. Women traditionally have been less free to move around in literal spatial terms than men because 'societies have generated their own rules, culturally determined, for making boundaries on the ground' (Ardener, 11–12). Janet Wolff identifies as 'the modern hero', the male figure of the *flaneur*, who has the 'freedom to move about in the city, observing and being observed' (39), sharing with 'the stranger' in male-authored writing 'the possibility and the prospect of lone travel, of voluntary uprooting, of anonymous arrival at a new place' (Wolff, 39). There is no precise fe-male equivalent of such figures in modern urban culture. Even in the early twentieth century it was not considered safe or acceptable for 'respectable' women to roam, but 'morally dangerous' (Pollock, 69). In *The Judge*, Ellen has happy memories of roving beyond Edinburgh with her mother and her school-friend Rachael Wing, but the difficulties for women wishing to enter the public space in a non-sexualised way are shown; Ellen and Mrs Melville, crossing the city at night on their way back from a walk, are followed by a man 'savouring the women's terror under his tongue' (11).

Among other things '. . . the suffrage struggle seemed to promise women some space of their own in the city, which was public, not private' (Marcus, 136), a space both physical and non-corporeal. The scenes in *The Judge* showing Ellen selling suffragette magazines and attending meetings where women make speeches, illustrate women's aspirations not only for the vote but for greater freedom asserted through the occupation of space and the rhetoric of suffragette activism, which 'defiantly infiltrated a normatively masculine domain of political rhetoric and argument' (Felski, 151). Yet so-ciety remained unconvinced; Ellen's own mother, using a variation on the popular late nineteenth-century term 'wild woman' (denoting 'the New Woman'), gives mild expression to the widely-held concern for propriety surrounding female behaviour in public places when she says to Richard Yaverland: 'I hope you don't think Ellen a wild girl, running about to these meetings all alone' (78). While many male-authored canonical modern paintings represent public spaces, 'the street, the bar, the cafe' (Pollock, 57), they frequently depict particular divisions in sexual roles, showing encounters 'between men who have the freedom to take their pleasures in many urban spaces and women from a class subject to them who have to work in those spaces often selling their bodies to clients, or to artists' (Pollock, 54). She may have sought new kinds of role, but 'to enter the public domain, the New Woman had to confront and avoid the label public woman ,which at the *fin de siècle* was synonymous with streetwalker ' (Ledger, 154).

West, illustrating the difficulties faced by women entering the public domain, also offers both a diagnosis of 'male sexual paranoia' in this novel as she does elsewhere in her fiction (Gilbert and Gubar, 98), and an exposure of hypocrisy. Philip James spots Ellen in the streets of Edinburgh with Richard: '"She's standing there making herself as conspicuous as if she were a street girl!" he screamed to himself' (123). Philip, watching Ellen and Richard voyeuristically, is approached by a girl; he 'hated her for being a streetwalker and for being taller than he, and began to swear at her . . . all these women were vile. There was no measure to the vileness that Ellen had brought on him' (125). But the reader learns that he has used a prostitute himself: 'It had been his belief that the advantage of prostitution was that it gave one command over women like Ellen without bringing on one the trouble that would certainly follow if one did ill to Ellen' (126).

The laws of society (enforced by Philip James) are shown interwoven with widely-held and contradictory moral and sexual attitudes. Ellen's awareness of state hypocrisy is heightened when she responds to a suffragette speaker's indictment of 'the double standard of morality and the treatment of unmarried mothers' (57). Ellen, although just seventeen, 'could not abide the State's pretence that an illegitimate baby had only one parent when everybody knew that every baby had really two' (57). Sexually innocent (and like the reader unaware of the future significance of such issues for her), she broods on the nature of 'some kind of embrace' that leads to babies:

> she had learned lately, too, that women who were very poor sometimes let men do this thing to them for money: such were the women whom

she saw in John Square, when she came back late from a meeting or a concert, leaning against the garden-railings, their backs to the lovely nocturnal mystery of groves and moonlit lawns, and their faces turned to the line of rich men's houses which mounted out of the night like a tall, impregnable fortress (57).

The representation of space here, with the image of the prostitutes in the public square and the powerful structures of prosperous patriarchy, foregrounds the economic factors influencing sexual behaviour, and draws attention to the inequalities of class and gender roles which are exposed, too, in Ellen's work situation.

Ellen's frustration in her workplace is powerfully imaged; chastised by Philip's father for 'hanging about with a man' (135), she is angry about the 'client' (actually Philip) who has complained. Looking out of the office window she thinks '[s]urely she had as much right in Princes Street as he had? And if it was too late for her to be there, then it was too late for him also. "It's just a case of one law for the man and another for the woman. Och, votes for women!" she cried savagely, and flogged the window with the blindcord' (137). The violence of her action suggests not only her anger at injustice, but her sense of constriction. She longs for travel and excitement (19), for the kind of freedom enjoyed by Richard Yaverland; whereas 'he could captain his ship through the steepest seas' (58), '[n]o going to sea for me', laments Ellen (106). As Richard walks the streets freely:

...her mind had to follow him in a kind of dream, as he walked on, masterfully, as one who knows he has the right to come and go, out of that wet grey street of which she was a part, to wander as he chose in strange continents, in exotic weathers, through time sequined with extravagant dawns and sunsets, through space jewelled with towns running red with blood of revolutions or multi–coloured with carnival (138).

Again, Ellen's vivid, violent vision strikingly suggests the force of her frustration and longing.

In Book II of the novel, too, the issue of women's relationship to public spaces is raised. Marion Yaverland resolves to make friends with Ellen: '"I will talk to her about the Suffragettes. What shall I say about them? I do honestly think that they are splendid women. I think there was never anything so fine as the way they go out into the streets knowing they will be stoned . . ." A memory overcame her' (262). It is soon revealed that

Marion herself has been stoned, not for suffragette activity, but for an il-
licit pregnancy. In a flashback, the reader shares her pain, walking through
public spaces pursued by men jeering and throwing missiles at her for her
sexual and social transgression (her lover being the Squire's son, Marion
breaks class boundaries). Near the end of the novel the character known
as 'Poppy Alicante' attracts Marion's sympathy; she recognises that Poppy
has probably borne a child to some 'handsome sailor' who 'picked her up
in Chatham High Street' (395). Poppy stimulates an image in Ellen's mind,
too: 'the tail of some memory of an open place round which women stood
looking just like this' (386). Later she understands: 'It was of nothing in
art she had been thinking, but of John Square in Edinburgh, where after
nightfall women had leaned against the garden railings . . .' (425). The 'fallen
woman', not merely an artistic image here as in male painting, haunts the
novel. *The Judge* exposes the way in which women at this period longed,
but were unable, to enjoy fully the freedom of public space; linked to this,
the double standards which applied, morally and socially, particularly in
sexual matters, are underlined.

The complexities of women's relationship to structures both literal and
social are also examined. For men, property, like the 'rich men's houses' in
John Square, is power, offering security to Philip James 'if only he had the
sense to stay in the district of orderly houses where he belonged' (126); his
fears of disintegration are calmed by thinking of 'the solidity of his father's
house' (127). Ellen, on the other hand, may unlock and open the door of
the shabby house she shares with her mother, 'as if she were the man of
the house' (44), but she does not have property-owner Richard Yaverland's
careless powers. It is poignant and ironic, too, that Mrs Melville, dying in
hospital, remarks to Ellen (predating Woolf) '. . . nice to have a room of
one's own' (184).

In the novel's second half, interior space is more fully examined.
Yaverland's End, Marion's home, is not, however, a safe domestic sphere.
Ellen's arrival there marks a shift in the novel from realism to something
more disturbing; she can be seen, Philip Ray argues, as an innocent heroine
entering a nightmarish Gothic Castle. Unlike Gothic castles, though, Marion
Yaverland's house is not a place of strict containment. Marion, since her
public stoning 'had felt fear at any contact with the external world' (286).
We learn she innocently admitted Peacey to her home, where he raped her,
and 'she wandered in the dark caverns of her mind' (287). Marion's home
has become in the Freudian sense, 'unhomely'. The rape is never publically
acknowledged, and Homi Bhabha's comment on the breach of the domestic space in several (other) modern novels highlights a subversive aspect of

West's text: '[b]y making visible the forgetting of the 'unhomely' moment in civil society, feminism specifies the patriarchal, gendered nature of civil society and disturbs the symmetry of private and public' (10–1).

Marion Yaverland's house breaks down boundaries. It is remarkably open to the surrounding landscape; Ellen feels uncomfortable in the new room built by Marion with its high windows, found by many people to be 'more like a lighthouse than a home' (240). There 'all who sat within were forced to look out on the windy firmament and see the earth spread far below' (241). Marion herself, wounded by her experiences, is described metaphorically in terms that link her to the dwelling: 'doubt was wandering from chamber to chamber of her being' (239). This second half of the novel, like 'a case history drawn from some psychiatrist's notebook' (Orel, 127), seems to map out a psychic rather than a social space, and a troubling one. Ellen 'knew she would find living on the ledge of this view quite intolerable' (241).

Marion's view is not, like that from the city window, on to a 'masculine' public space, but on to a landscape. In the novel's first half, the Pentland hills offer Ellen freedom and spiritual release, being seen by Richard as emblematic of Ellen herself (106). Despite being linked to a woman, seeming 'curiously like Marion' (232), the Essex landscape is different in character and function. A flat marshy plain described as 'this new and curious estate of nature, this substance that was neither earth nor water, this place that was neither land nor sea' (231), it appears highly symbolic. This landscape, giving 'in its brightness some indication of its sucking softness' (231) seems feminine, maternal: '[i]t had its own strange scenery; it had its undulations and its fissures, and between deep, rounded, shining banks, a course marked here and there by the stripped white ghosts of sapling trees' (231–2).

The actual maternal body, hinted at here metaphorically, is described in a positive way at Mrs Melville's deathbed, and '[t]he daughter's flesh, touching the mother's, remembered life in the womb, that loving organ that by night and day does not cease to embrace its beloved' (185). This can be related to Julia Kristeva's idea of the 'semiotic', the 'pre-Oedipal, early phase in a child's existence' when 'its physical experience is part of a continuum with the maternal body' (Morris,144). It can be argued, on this basis, that 'the figure of the mother becomes the basic signifying space for the regenerative cycle' (Scott, 133). The landscape associated with Marion, a mother, 'had a solemn quality of importance. It was as if this was the primeval ooze from which the first life stirred and crawled landwards to begin to make this a memorable star' (*The Judge*, 232). According to Scott, '[t]he marsh as regenerative site bears comparison to the pond, whose muddy depths generate the words for the future drama of Woolf's *Between the Acts*' (1995, 136).

However, Marion's landscape can also be read less affirmatively. Marshlands are associated by Richard Yaverland earlier in the novel with women: '[t]hey stood at the edge of the primeval swamps and called the men down from the highlands of civilisation and certain cells determined upon immortality betrayed their victims to them' (71). Although Richard is shown as misogynistic (it is he who pulls down Ellen from 'the highlands of civilisation') and mud is associated with Philip James too (135), a troubling, deterministic view of women's roles arguably lingers through the novel.

Marion chooses solitude, largely rejecting human society and its institutions in a way that Ellen finds terrifying (247). In her almost timeless location, where 'there would be no illusion that anything happens suddenly or that anything disappears' (228), Marion places herself outside what Kristeva terms the 'symbolic order' of society: '[w]e cannot gain access to the temporal scene, that is, to the political and historical affairs of our society, except by identifying with the values considered to be masculine (mastery, superego, the sanctioning communicative word that institutes stable social exchange)' (Kristeva, 155). Marion's 'lighthouse' room, so open to the 'maternal' landscape, suggests the way in which she is open to the unconscious drives, termed by Kristeva the 'call of the mother'(156), which pre-exist the symbolic order in the human psyche. Marion finally entirely rejects the 'masculine values' of the symbolic order which sustains social identity, and in doing so, like Kristeva's mother-identified woman, 'leaves herself unprotected and open to the full force of unconscious desire, of which the most powerful is always the death drive. A desire to return to the mother can become a desire for loss of identity, for a dissolution of self in m/other - for death' (Morris, 148). Marion's final note reads ' [t]his is the end. Death. Death. Death '(423), and she dies entering the sea as Edna Pontellier had done in Kate Chopin's *The Awakening*. Here, as in the American novel, there is a tracing of 'the working of the death instinct once the barrier of social identity is breached' (Morris, 150). At the end, Richard stands 'looking out to the east, to the open sea, over the country of the mud. He was thinking of Marion, and wondering where the tide had carried her. The inexorable womb was continuing to claim its own' (430).

'At times . . . in her writing Kristeva is open to the criticism that in austerely refusing a consolatory myth of a nurturing utopian pre-Oedipal mother she falls for the opposing myth of an engulfing, annihilating mother, an image we are familiar with in many male-authored texts' (Morris, 148); such a charge might also be levelled at West's idea of 'the inexorable womb' and the absolute terms of the epigraph '[e]very mother is a judge who sentences the children for the sins of the father' (346). In *The Judge* West arguably assigns rigid gendered roles: suffering and guilt for women, death for Marion and a trap for Ellen, once so lively and political. Men, for their part, are identified with destruction and betrayal: Richard Yaverland is a munitions expert; Peacey, Marion's rapist, is ironically named; Philip James betrays Ellen; Mactavish James had betrayed Isabella Kingan (significantly, West's mother was called Isabella); Harry had betrayed Marion. Ellen broods, on her mother's death, that 'this was a frightening universe to live in, when the laws of nature behaved like very lawless men' (189).

Yet the experience of reading the novel is complicated. *The Judge*, with its 'exploration of the constraints and restrictions experienced by women in a patriarchal culture', the ways in which women are 'sentenced to containment and silence' (Wolff, 10), should not be hastily judged. Marion's passionate love for the child Richard is both affecting and disturbing, her character both appealing and appalling. The shifting point of view unsettles any simple response, with the reader sometimes sharing a male perspective. Although it has aspects difficult for modern readers, such as the interest in eugenics and the handling of class (handsome Richard is the son of the squire, Roger the weakling, the butler's son), this novel is immensely powerful and suggestive. West resisted H.G.Wells' wish for her to compress *The Judge*, arguing 'I don't see why you can't have rich complex beauty '(Glendinning 1988, 81), and the novel's metaphorical construction, visual qualities and rich language invite plural readings. West's fiction not only presents a challenge to its society, but, read in the context of ideas about the 'feminine sentence' articulated most famously by Virginia Woolf (Pykett 90–111), can be seen as making its own contribution to debates about gender and literary form in the modern period.

Works Cited

Ardener, Shirley 'Ground Rules and Social Maps for Women: An Introduction' in *Women and Space*. Shirley Ardener ed. London: Croom Helm, 1981, 11–34
Bhaba, Homi *The Location of Culture*. London: Routledge, 1994
Felski, Rita *The Gender of Modernity*.Cambridge, Massachusetts and London: Harvard University Press, 1995

Gilbert, Sandra M and Susan Gubar *No Man's Land: The Place of the Woman Writer in the Twentieth Century.* vol. 1. New Haven and London: Yale University Press, 1988

Gish, Nancy K. See MacDiarmid, Hugh, below

Glendinning, Victoria *Rebecca West: A Life.* 1987; London: Papermac, 1988

Glendinning, Victoria 'Introduction' to Rebecca West *Harriet Hume.* 1929; London: Virago, 1980

Kristeva, Julia *The Kristeva Reader.* Toril Moi ed.Oxford: Basil Blackwell, 1986

Ledger, Sally *The New Woman: Fiction and Feminism at the Fin de Siècle.* Manchester: Manchester University Press, 1997

MacDiarmid, Hugh 'Following Rebecca West in Edinburgh: A Monologue in the Vernacular', *Scottish Chapbook* 1 June 1922; reference here to reprint in *The Gender of Modernism: A Critical Anthology.* Bonnie Kime Scott ed. Bloomington and Indianopolis: Indiana University Press, 1990, 275–86, with an introduction by Nancy K. Gish

MacDiarmid, Hugh 'Newer Scottish Fiction (1)', *Scottish Educational Journal.* 25 June 1926. Reprint in *Contemporary Scottish Studies.* Edinburgh: Scottish Educational Journals, 1976, 108–9

Marcus, Jane 'A Wilderness of One's Own: Feminist Fantasy Novels of the Twenties: Rebecca West and Sylvia Townsend Warner' in *Women Writers and the City: Essays in Feminist Literary Criticism.* Susan Merrill Squier ed. Knoxville: University of Tennessee, 1984, 134–60

Morris, Pam. *Literature and Feminism.* Oxford: Basil Blackwell, 1993

Norton, Ann 'Rebecca West's Ironic Heroine: Beauty as Tragedy in *The Judge*', *Literature in Transition 1880–1920.* vol. 34, no. 3. 1991, 294–308

Orel, Harold *The Literary Achievement of Rebecca West.* New York: St Martin's Press, 1986

Pollock, Griselda 'Modernity and Spaces of Femininity' in *Vision and Difference: Femininity, Feminism and Histories of Art.* Griselda Pollock ed. London: Routledge, 1988, 54–78

Pykett, Lyn *Engendering Fictions: The English Novel in the Early Twentieth Century.* London: Edward Arnold, 1995

Ray, Philip *The Judge* Reexamined: Rebecca West's Underrated Gothic Romance', *English Literature in Transition 1880–1920.* vol. 31, no 3. 1988, 297–307

Scott, Bonnie Kime *Refiguring Modernism, Volume 2: Postmodern Feminist Readings of Woolf, West, and Barnes.* Bloomington and Indianapolis: Indiana University Press, 1995

Stevenson, Robert Louis *The Strange Case of Dr Jekyll and Mr Hyde* and *Weir of Hermiston*. Emma Letley ed. 1886, 1896; Oxford: Oxford University Press, 1987

Stevenson, Robert Louis *Edinburgh: Picturesque Notes*. 1873; Edinburgh: Salamander Press, 1987

Tickner, Lisa *The Spectacle of Woman: Imagery of the Suffrage Campaign 1907–14*. London: Chatto and Windus, 1987.

West, Rebecca *The Judge*. 1922; London: Virago, 1980

West, Rebecca *Family Memories*. Faith Evans ed. 1987; London: Lime Tree, 1992

Wolff, Janet *Feminine Sentences: Essays on Women and Culture*. Oxford: Polity Press, 1990

Nan Shepherd (1893–1981)

Nan Shepherd was born in 1893 in West Cults, Deeside, and spent the majority of her life there. She studied at Aberdeen University, graduating from King's College in 1915. For the next forty one years she worked as a lecturer in English at Aberdeen College of Education. While Shepherd was involved in literary activities throughout her life, her three novels *The Quarry Wood* (1928), *The Weatherhouse* (1930) and *A Pass in the Grampians* (1933) were published in a burst of creative activity and met with critical acclaim both in Britain and the United States. Shepherd continued to write articles and reviews and numbered among her friends Neil Gunn, Hugh MacDiarmid, Willa Muir and Jessie Kesson. She was also a friend of the poet Charles Murray of whose poems she wrote an appreciation in 1969, and of Agnes Mure Mackenzie, publishing a portrait of her in 1955. She edited the *Aberdeen University Review* for seven years in the fifties and sixties and was awarded an honorary degree by the University in 1964. While always returning to her family home in West Cults, Shepherd travelled extensively. She was also a keen hill walker, an interest reflected in her collection of poems *In the Cairngorms* (1934) and in a nonfiction piece *The Living Mountain* (1977; reprinted 1997). While Shepherd's novels were out of print for many years, critical interest in them has been revived since their republication in the 1980s and 1990s. Nan Shepherd died in 1981.

Alison Lumsden

Boundaries and Transgression in Nan Shepherd's *The Quarry Wood*

Gillian Carter

The fence was not neglected from carelessness, or procrastination, or a distaste for work. Still less, of course, from indifference. Miss Leggatt had a tender concern for her seedlings, and would interrupt even a game of cards at the advent of a scraping hen. But deep within herself she felt obscurely the contrast between the lifeless propriety of a fence and the lively interest of shooing a hen; and Aunt Josephine at every turn chose instinctively the way of life (1987, 4).

This passage from *The Quarry Wood* speaks of a gentle anarchy in a world governed by property and propriety. Chasing a hen provides movement across an imagined boundary; a fence physically constructs separation and division. By taking this focus on the fence/boundary as an enabling metaphor, *The Quarry Wood* can be constructed as a text which resists attempts to constrain it within those frameworks seeking to promote a single, essential meaning.

The Quarry Wood may well be read as a classic development novel which follows the growth to intellectual and emotional maturity of its heroine, Martha Ironside, and her struggle to achieve an autonomous identity in a world governed by male values (Watson, 1990, 209), but it is more complex than this. Identity in a post-Freudian world is not straightforward and the search for an autonomous identity can be read as a patriarchal ideal. Shepherd deconstructs this ideal in *The Quarry Wood* by breaking the convention of the unified, autonomous self associated with patriarchal society in her construction of character, landscape and community, and the narrative itself. The exploration of Martha's pursuit of knowledge, her relation to home and community, and the discovery of her passionate nature shows the unified self with defined boundaries to be a delusion. This is the process which shapes *The Quarry Wood*.

There are many possible ways of reading *The Quarry Wood*; this essay is only one and a necessarily partial one. The reading focuses on the construction of identity by utilising the play of binary opposites apparent in the character of Martha. These primarily consist of the oppositions subject/object, mind/body, culture/nature and Scottish/English. Meaning is gained by the positive/centre/male defining against and repressing its opposite, the negative/female/margin. Briefly, binary opposites can be read both horizontally and vertically, with the associative power of the vertical reading encoding notions of superiority and inferiority in all forms of Western discourse. In her famous passage from 'Sorties' in *The Newly Born Woman*, Hélène Cixous writes, 'through dual, hierarchical oppositions . . . . Everywhere (where) ordering intervenes, where a law organizes what is thinkable by oppositions (dual, irreconcilable; or sublatable, dialectical)' (1994, 38). The works of Nan Shepherd contain these dualisms. However, since binarisms are not polarised in Shepherd but constantly interact, they also encode different constructions of identity to the official, authoritative versions. The space between the opposites is the site for the production of meaning.

The novel has been described as indicating 'the necessary balance of inner and outer existences; of body and spirit, self and world' (Smith, 1988, 53). This reading echoes Watson's in its articulation of an essential, identifiable subject position which disregards the competing psychological and ideological forces which contribute to the construction of identity. Balance implies stasis and equality where there is actually movement and growth, change and power shifts. Balance, too, has associations of the rational, logical, masculine side of the oppositions: the very oppositions Martha has to come to terms with. However, if we take the character of Martha as the site for the production of meaning, we can read *The Quarry Wood* as a text which resists the finality of the humanist construction of identity and, instead, constructs a self that is *in process*.

Luke, Martha's love interest and best friend's husband, describes Martha as 'so absolutely herself . . . . So still and self-contained too' (49). While Martha appears self-contained in her singularity, the narrative voice reminds the reader that the self cannot be severed from the outside world, 'She had not yet discovered that men and women are of importance in the scheme of things' (51), 'the importance of things lies not in themselves but in their relations' (149). Evelyn Fox Keller refers to this as the 'objectivist illusion':

The objectivist illusion reflects back an image of self as autonomous and objectified: an image of individuals unto themselves, severed from the outside world of other objects (animate as well as inanimate) and simultaneously from their own subjectivity (1985, 70).

This brings forward the subject/object dichotomy, and the movement between the two, which governs Martha's development in the novel. Martha, believing herself to be in love with Luke, becomes the personification of his spiritual desires at the expense of her material existence as a woman; '[s]he was the spirit made visible in the flesh; tangible thought. He forgot that she was alive' (84). She internalises Luke's vision of her ('He made her great by believing her so' [76]) until she begins to learn the difference between knowledge and wisdom, and read the world with a fuller understanding:

And she smiled a bitter mirth. 'I'm an uncompleted work of art. My creator has flung me aside.' But stung suddenly by the admission the thought implied, Good Lord!' she exclaimed. 'Am I such a slave as that? Dependent on a man to complete me! I thought I couldn't be anything without him – I can be my own creator' (184).

Up to this point, Martha is so absorbed by her pursuit of knowledge that she disregards the material side of her existence. The contact with the external world is there but she has forgotten that people are 'intersubjectively constituted and interconnected' (Burrows, 1996, 10). The realisation of self-delusion enables Martha to cease perceiving herself as object and begin the process of discovering her own subjectivity.

The construction of Martha's relationship with Luke is just one example of the varied techniques Shepherd uses to emphasise the non-fixity of identity. The point of view slides between character and narrator, achieving its irony by counterpointing them and emphasising the limitations of Martha's perspective. Part of Martha's 'getting of wisdom' is learning to see this multiplicity of perspectives:

Late at night a fierce clarity came into her thoughts. She saw all that had chanced in the last two years sort itself into patterns. The patterns shifted; no two were quite alike, yet all were recognizably the same; and it seemed to her that she was looking in succession at the events of her life through the eyes of all the different actors in them (158).

The shifting subject position enables a composite picture to be drawn through partial and situated knowledge, and the focus on the other characters places Martha in relation to her community and complicates any sense of self.

Shepherd's technique draws attention to the multiplicity of the text, through the character of Martha as well as in her construction of the narrative, the structure of which breaks away from traditional forms. The narrative moves forward by a method of undercutting and digression. So, while the narrative appears linear, it is able to convey a multiplicity of perspectives and provides a sense of fluidity. Absolute closure cannot be achieved because of the variety of discourses, voices and speaking positions that are at work in the novel, and because of the incidentally offered information that is beyond the scope of the text (such as Roy's proposal in Martha's future). This culminates in the ambiguous ending (frustrating to some critics) which is one of the modernist characteristics exemplified by the novel.

The narrative itself is carried by culture/nature connections; the passage of time is conveyed through the school and university terms, and the changing seasons commented on by Geordie, uniting the natural and the cultural worlds. Movement between the oppositions also occurs within the story itself: the portrayal of Aunt Josephine putting her broom aside to watch the child, Martha, dancing as a clumsy star is juxtaposed by the immutable law of housework in her sister Jean Corbett's household (9), setting natural forces beside the cultural law of respectability.

Notions of expansion and containment are also inscribed in the relationship between culture and nature. The idea of containment is woven into the landscape:

> Shapes, sounds, the energies and acutenesses of life, were muffled in the dull white that covered both earth and sky. No sun came through. The weeks dragged on with no lifting of the pallor. The snow melted a little and froze again with smears of dirt marbling its surfaces. To the northward of the dykes it was lumped in obstinate seams, at the cottage doors trodden and caked, matted with refuse, straws and stones and clots of dung carried in about on clorted boots (60).

Descriptions of the physical world contrast with Martha's absorption in her intellectual and spiritual worlds, and are set in counterpoint to the cramped conditions of her home life. Houses are important: the domestic space constricts Martha, her foster-sister, Madge, suffocates her, and her world is bounded by external, material reality.

The narrative moves between these internal and external realities and also explores the sense of a widening world. In chapter six, 'Expansion of the World', Martha is going to university for the first time, and experiences an expansion in space and geography. Listening to Professor Gregory's lecture on English Literature, she also expands her intellectual horizons; she discovers 'new countries . . . undiscovered country that awaited her conquest' (52). Conquest is important here. For the first time, Martha is offered a real chance at power in the possibility of intellectual challenge. Here Martha must confront the concept of mastery. The search for knowledge and the various forms it can assume is a central theme of *The Quarry Wood* and is integral to Martha's emotional and intellectual development.

In this sense, gently anarchic Aunt Josephine is Martha's greatest teacher because 'it was she that taught her wisdom; thereby proving - she [Martha] reflected - that man does not learn from books alone' (1). But it is Josephine that places the greatest burden on Martha by refusing all forms of home-help or nursing aid while she is ill. The lesson, however, is in the caring. Val Plumwood writes, 'The experience of resistance the real world offers to the self is obtained through the encounter with someone else's needs and reality, creating an interactive process in which each transforms and limits the other' (1993, 156). The egocentric requirements of Martha's pursuit of knowledge are re-shaped by the sacrifices she makes for Aunt Josephine. In assuming a caring role for both Josephine and, later, Robin, Martha comes to terms with her own fragmented self:

> She had no idea she could be so masterful. Something of the security of handling Robin seemed to have passed into her relations with other folk. Her old diffidence was gone. The current of her life was running strong and sure; but underground; deeper as yet than her own knowledge (197).

Implications for change and growth are inscribed in the sense of movement and time, and the natural metaphor for Martha's self is placed in relation to the cultural importance of her place in a community.

For much of the novel, Martha sees institutional knowledge as more valuable than the wisdom embodied in Aunt Josephine and Geordie. She pursues this knowledge as one would a lover; 'She had learned as yet to be passionate on behalf of one thing only – knowledge: but for that she could intrigue like any lover' (31). 'She snatched because she lived in fever. Greedy, convulsive, in a jealous agony, she raced for knowledge, panting' (50). Her denial of the material world, and her physical existence within it, is channelled to this end. The boundary between mind and body is blurred by the sexual metaphor for Martha's search for knowledge. Keller shows how the two can be conflated:

> Knowledge is a form of consummation, just as sex is a form of knowledge. Both are propelled by desire. Whether in fantasy, experience or linguistic trope, sexual union remains the most compelling and most primal instance of the act of knowing. Even when unrecognized by metaphor, the experience of knowing is rooted in the carnal. It does not, however, remain there. What classically distinguishes knowledge is its essential thrust away from the body: its ambition to transcend the carnal. Mind is not simply immanent in matter; it is transcendent over it (18).

Keller encapsulates the classic struggle for dominance between the mind and the body. 'Thrust', 'ambition' and 'transcendent' are all terms which are associated with the masculine, 'mind' side of the oppositions. In a world which posits these as desirable, Martha attempts to escape the confines of her gendered, 'embodied' role and live in the public institutional arena at the expense of the private, domestic sphere. The transcendence of the mind, however, cannot be achieved because the boundary between the mind and the body keeps moving within the relationship of their necessary interdependence.

As Gayatri Spivak points out, the public is woven out of the private and, consequently, the private always has 'public potential' (1987, 103). The private/domestic side intrudes – often rudely – on the public/culture side; home life disrupts study, the body intrudes on the mind. Martha's confusing of her physical love for Luke by placing it on the same plane as her search for knowledge is shown to be a delusion upon the revelations of her family's unpleasant neighbour, Stoddart Semple; '[a]nd what was love really like? Not so sheerly spiritual after all. She recalled the frenzy of her June desire' (159). The private, material world of the body disrupts her esoteric romanticism, undermining the privileged position attributed to the mind in Martha's search for self-knowledge. Reconciliation of the split between the two, then, denotes the reaching of some sort of understanding rather than balance, an understanding that is still open to reassessment and/or change.

Taking this a step further, the novel can be read as foregrounding issues of Scottishness and Englishness and, as with the binarisms of culture and nature, and public and private, slides between the two, eliding essential definition. Because of the relationship between history, language and landscape, we are able to read certain texts as 'belonging' to a particular region, as 'speaking' from a particular position, of 'constructing' a particular place:

> Martha said it over and over to herself: *Scotland is bounded on the south by England, on the east by the rising sun, on the north by the Arory-bory-Alice, and on the west by eternity.*
> Eternity did not seem to be in any of her maps: but neither was the Aurora. She accepted that negligence of the map-makers as she accepted so much else in life. She had enough to occupy her meanwhile in discovering what life held, without concerning herself as to what it lacked (20).

Surrounded on three sides by forces infinite and mystical, Scotland lies on the edge of the mapped world, defined by its proximity to England on its fourth. This would suggest that England alone anchors Scotland in the material world. Scotland, it would appear, can only be read in relation to England because the other boundaries are not charted in atlases. They belong to other discourses which are not contained by the map-making process. This does not mean, however, that they are not there: the narrator states that the negligence is on the part of the map-makers and not in the reality Martha experiences. There is a contrast between imaginative and material boundaries, between what can be reasonably seen and what is imaginatively experienced. Scotland can be read as linking the material and the spiritual, a split which is embodied, then reconciled, in Martha.

This idea can be seen in Shepherd's use of the languages of Scotland. All her novels have a predominantly English narrative interspersed with Scots terminology and phrasing, and specifically north eastern Scots:

> Mary Annie's man was dead. He had died three months after getting a complete set of false teeth. Unlucky all the ways of it, those teeth. He hadn't had them three weeks when he had a drop too much. Some late in coming home, he was, and not so able to hold his liquor as he used to be . . . 'an' him spewin' a' the road hame, in ahin dykes an' sic-like' (45).

Yet while English appears to dominate, the narrative, in fact, modulates between Scots and English. The language issue, however, becomes more complex when examined in relation to the character of Martha. In the early chapters of *The Quarry Wood*, we see the child, Martha, speak Scots. As she gets older and pursues her education, she speaks English. While modern Anglo-Scots is comfortably recreated in the narrative voice, the contrast of the north-east Scots speech of the major rural characters to Martha's English is, at first, problematic. The critic Margaret Elphinstone finds the ending frustrating because she believes Martha's fragmentation, as exemplified in the English of her education and the Scots of her background, can never be reconciled. She says that 'Martha is shown to sacrifice a part of herself. This is shown in the division between Scots and English which gives linguistic form to the division within Martha herself' (1993, 31). The passage Elphinstone chooses to exemplify her point is appropriate. Here, Martha is attempting to complete a Latin exercise in order to compete for a bursary. She intends to go to university but this is not yet public knowledge. In the warmth, dirt, bustle and play, her ink is spilt over the exercise:

> 'Blaudin' ma towel an' a',' she [Emmeline] grumbled; and then,
> 'Ye micht dicht it up,' she said to Martha.
> Martha gulped. She suddenly wanted to scream, to cry out at the pitch of her voice, 'I haven't time, I haven't time, I haven't time! What's a kitchen table in comparison with my Latin, with knowing things, with catching up on the interminable past! There isn't *time!*' (27).

Elphinstone continues, 'The language echoes the thought expressed, Scots against English, a kitchen table against a Latin exercise.' These splits, however, are complicated in ways that, at first, are not clearly evident. As Elphinstone points out, the division between the public world of institutionalised education and the private world of Martha's home life is reflected in the Scots/English linguistic division. Martha, however, ultimately chooses to remain in the domestic world of her home and take on the upbringing of the baby, Robin, yet retains her Anglicised speech and her work as a primary school teacher in the public world. Concepts of language and silence too, provide cause for rethinking the more obvious divisions. Martha is silent in both the public and private worlds until, through Robin, she finds voice and strength by drawing on oral traditions in her singing and storytelling traditions rooted firmly in Scottish culture.

Elphinstone feels that Shepherd's relation to Scots is as ambiguous as her character, Martha's. This is particularly evidenced, she claims, by Shepherd's tendency to put some, but not all, Scots words in italics. Elphinstone states that italics shows the author's distance from the words. However, the italics can be read as an act of interpretation or explanation; 'the Post-colonial writer whose gaze is turned in two directions, stands already in that position which will come to be occupied by an interpretation, for he/she is not the object of an interpretation, but the first interpreter' (Ashcroft et al, 1989, 61). Rather than reading the act of italicising as ambiguous, the italicisation of certain words can be read as a reflection of the author's position in relation to the language, for Shepherd is certainly gazing in two directions, standing, as she does, at the nexus of two cultures.

This position is inscribed in Martha. She is located in the position where identity and national identity are imbricated. The moment when Martha is shown to gaze out at the view with some authority exemplifies this position and is further complicated by questions of gender:

> 'Come and look at Lochnagar', she answered. And when he scrambled down from his eyrie and came to the garden gate, from which they could see the long panorama of the hills, she said, softly, as though her voice might smudge the pale shimmering beauty of the morning, 'Distance upon distance. Wouldn't you think it would never end?'
>
> 'Wait till you've seen the Veld,' he said. His loud cheerful voice seemed to roll echoing about in the empty morning. 'You won't talk about distances then. Or going down to Delagoa – the low Veld. You look down and down and there's always more of it. You begin to think it must be the sea and it isn't. It's always more earth' (147).

Here we have a male colonial/coloniser imposing his view of a landscape over that of an indigenous female. His mastery is revealed through his voice: loud, confident, cheerful; her voice is soft, gentle, careful. Voice and landscape are linked, with Roy's story dominating Martha's. Roy's wooing of Martha is likened to claiming a little portion of Scotland, 'and already, after a couple of hours in Crannochie he was stretching out his hand to claim a little portion of the world that he found there. That portion was Martha' (145), and, as in the colonisation of homeland, he retains the spirit of the coloniser and takes the woman as the nation, reading woman and landscape in his own terms, refusing the possibility of other stories.

Shepherd, however, is not representing the landscape as feminised, and the coloniser/colonised position is not entirely gender-specific. While 'femi-nine connectedness with and passivity toward nature' (Plumwood, 22–23) is generally presented as the norm, in *The Quarry Wood*, Geordie is the character most closely connected to the land, not in the sense of masculine domination but as something weary, elemental and basic. Martha's connection with the land starts with Josephine but is ultimately achieved through her father:

> And once she had a far off glimpse of Geordie, in a steep field some distance from the road. She watched the horses straining up the furrow, back and neck one rigid line. She watched them turn. Then horses and plough and man were swallowed up in the darkness at the far end of the field, against the upturned earth and the blur of wood. Only when the team swung round and their white foreheads and noses glimmered through the brown could she distinguish where they were. It was surely impossible that Geordie could see longer to cut the furrow; but his eyes had been bent so long upon the darkness of the earth that he seemed to share its life, know his way with it by touch. Martha brooded, her eyes on the slow sombre darkening; then lifted them and saw the arch of the sky. When she looked again her father and his team were blotted out, one with the earth.
>
> She thought, 'I've come from him.' She too was at one with the earth (204).

Martha's position in relation to the landscape is one of standing at ground level looking out and upward. The landscape portrayed is not undifferentiated and ahistorical; Martha's view is partial, limited by her position and the darkening sky, made into personal history by her own relation to it and that of her father's. The boundaries are blurred by the darkness and movement.

The boundaries maintained by traditional definitions of identity and nationality are also blurred. Just as identity cannot be fixed in Martha, national identity cannot be fixed in the text and, because *The Quarry Wood* is a text which invites multiple readings from various positions, it too cannot be fixed to a single, essential meaning. Reading *The Quarry Wood* with particular attention to binarisms enables the reader to take into account the simultaneous, but often contradictory, intersection of differences and how they inform, consciously and unconsciously, all readings of the text. Any one of the differences can take on more significance than the others; they are not equally weighted but constantly interact and reshape each other in a process that accepts contradiction, movement and change. The deconstruction of the fence – the transgression of the boundary – is central to this reading practice. This can be achieved by transferring the emphasis to what is considered marginal and, in the process, forcing movement of the boundary. By focusing on the deconstruction of binary opposites, we can read the character of Martha as the site of struggle between self and community, mind and body, and concepts of Scottishness and Englishness.

Works Cited

Ashcroft, Bill; Griffiths, Gareth; Tiffin, Helen. *The Empire Writes Back: Theory and Practice in Post-Colonial Literatures*. London: Routledge, 1989

Burrows, Victoria. 'Knowing Other People: An Interview With Lorraine Code', *Outskirts: Feminisms Along the Edge*. vol.1. May 1996, 8–10

Cixous, Hélène. 'Sorties', *The Newly Born Woman*, in *The Hélène Cixous Reader*. Susan Sellers ed. Betsy Wing trans. 1975; 1986; London & New York: Routledge, 1994, 37–45

Elphinstone, Margaret. 'Four Pioneering Novels', *Chapman*. no. 74–5. Autumn/Winter 1993, 23–9

Keller, Evelyn Fox. *Reflections on Gender and Science*. New Haven & London: Yale University Press, 1985

Plumwood, Val. *Feminism and the Mastery of Nature*. London & New York: Routledge, 1993

Shepherd, Nan. *The Quarry Wood*. 1928; Edinburgh: Canongate, 1987

Smith, Alison. Review of *The Quarry Wood* and *Imagined Corners*, *Scottish Literary Journal*. Supplement no. 28. Spring 1988, 52–4

Spivak, Gayatri Chakravorty. 'Explanation and Culture: Marginalia', *In Other Worlds: Essays in Cultural Politics*. London & New York: Methuen, 1987, 103–7

Watson, Roderick. '"... to get leave to live." Patterns of Identity, Freedom and Defeat in the Fiction of Nan Shepherd', *Studies in Scottish Fiction: Twentieth Century*. Joachim Schwend and Horst W Drescher eds. Frankfurt am Main: Peter Lang, 1990, 207–18

Journey into Being:
Nan Shepherd's *The Weatherhouse*

Alison Lumsden

Towards the end of *The Quarry Wood* Martha Ironside, finally released
from her obsession with Luke, realises that she can be her 'own creator'
(184). We might reasonably expect that in Shepherd's second novel, *The
Weatherhouse*, she will explore models of feminine identity available to a
woman who has taken her destiny into her own hands. Recent criticism has,
moreover, implied that such a concern with both gender and regional identity is a recurrent theme for Scottish writers. Christopher Whyte suggests
that because national identity is always problematic in minority cultures
they are 'privileged sites for the study of gender and its interaction with
other factors in the formation of identity' (1995, xvi). David Hewitt comments that a concern with regional identity 'might be said to be the generic
subject of regional literature' (1995, 190). The work of Nan Shepherd is
located geographically in the north-east – a region of the country which
Hewitt suggests adds its own particular resonances to Scottish identity – and
temporally in the Scottish Renaissance whose writers, Cairns Craig argues,
are marked by 'the restlessness of their search for a stable identity to the
Scotland they were trying to express' (1987, 7). As such Shepherd's work
would seem to offer a particularly fruitful area of study for those interested
in both Scottish and feminine identity.

It is within the world of the Weatherhouse, with its generations of Lorimer and Craigmyle women, that we might expect to uncover constructions
of feminine identity if they are to be found in the text. Indeed, there is
a sense in which Lindsay Lorimer – the youngest of its inhabitants – has
been sent there in order to construct her adult self in preparation for marriage. However, weather, for Shepherd, is a concept which does not fix
experience but unsettles it, revealing the multifaceted nature of perception.

A life-long hillwalker, Shepherd describes the effects of mist on the hills in her philosophical description of the Cairngorms, *The Living Mountain*:

> Such illusions, depending on how the eye is placed and used, drive home the truth that our habitual vision of things is not necessarily right: it is only one of an infinite number, and to glimpse an unfamiliar one, even for a moment, unmakes us, but steadies us again. It's queer but invigorating. It will take a long time to get to the end of a world that behaves like this if I do no more than turn round on my side or my back (1977; 1996, 78–9).

Consequently, the Weatherhouse – and by implication the novel which takes its name from it – is not a site where models of identity – either Scottish or feminine – are to be easily found. Rather, 'all corners and windows'(5), the house is a kaleidoscope through which we are offered a series of perspectives on the location of the feminine in an infinitely complex and problematic world.

In recent years feminist thought (particularly in its European manifestations) has suggested that there are, in fact, problems inherent for feminism in the very notion of identity itself. Julia Kristeva argues that the concept is bound up with entry into an essentially patriarchal 'symbolic order', suggesting that it is only with a rupture from the pre-signifying, and principally feminine space of the 'semiotic' that identity – the speaking subject – may be constructed:

> It requires an identification; in other words, the subject must separate from and through his image, from and through his objects. The image and objects must first be posited in a space that becomes symbolic because it connects the two separated positions, recording them or redistributing them in an open combinational system (1986, 98).

Clearly, this reveals a dichotomy at the very heart of feminine identity; a dichotomy not altogether resolved by Shepherd at the end of *The Quarry Wood* in spite of Martha's moment of self-realisation. If identity is dependant upon location within an essentially patriarchal space – the space inhabited by 'the Law' – how may woman position herself without collusion with a symbolic order essentially detrimental to her? On the other hand, if the feminine attempts location outside the social/symbolic order (and this may not be entirely possible) is this not simply to be positioned in an untenable location of perpetual opposition?

> If what woman desires is the very opposite of the sublimating Word and paternal legislation, she neither *has* nor *is* that opposite. All that remains for her is to pit herself constantly against that opposite in the very movement by which she desires it, to kill it repeatedly and then suffer endlessly (Kristeva, 1986, 144).

In Shepherd's text, similar questions about space and location are built into the construction of the Weatherhouse itself. Andrew Findlater's dilemma was one of how to tie together two mis–aligned cottages. Leeb resolves it by building an 'elfin' room, a 'quaint irregular hexagon' (5) (and she has the money to do so, a reminder that many problems may be simply economic). Designed to solve a spatial problem, the Weatherhouse thus encapsulates dichotomies about location inherent to its all-female community. Positioned within it, its inhabitants are both contained in isolation by its tower-like rooms and glass structure, and, as its 'protruding windows became part of the infinite world' (8), offered views to the wider perspectives beyond.

One perspective which may be seen from the windows of the Weatherhouse is the landscape surrounding Fetter-Rothnie. In *The Living Mountain* Shepherd writes that 'light in Scotland has a quality I have not met elsewhere. It is luminous without being fierce, penetrating to immense distances with an effortless intensity' (1977, 2). It is this same light which suffuses the landscape of *The Weatherhouse* in Shepherd's descriptions of dark, shadow, light and climate. However, such descriptions are not, as they sometimes are in north-east writers, merely lyrical, but serve a tropic function in the text, linking the world surrounding the Weatherhouse to an arena of experience beyond the purely social. Thus it is experienced by Garry Forbes who, first perceiving his return to the countryside as entry into a dead place in comparison to the world of the trenches, is suddenly seized by a new perspective:

> But as he mounted farther into the night, the night, growing upon his consciousness, was a dark hole no longer. The sky, still dark, brooded upon a darker earth, but with no sense of oppression. Rather both sky and earth rolled away, were lost in a primordial darkness whence they had but half emerged. Garry felt himself fall, ages of time gave way, and he too, was a creature only half set free from the primordial dark.

He was astonished at this effect upon himself, at the vastness which
this familiar country had assumed (56).

The repeated reference to the landscape as 'primordial' (both here and
elsewhere) serves to link it to an elemental area of experience outside the
concerns of men and history. Here 'time and the individual' (essentially
patriarchal constructions) are dissolved in light and space (the properties
of the feminine and semiotic) (58).

Given this tropic alignment of the landscape around Fetter-Rothnie to
what we might loosely describe as a 'semiotic' arena, it is hardly surprising
that Garry should be perplexed by his return to it from the trenches. Garry
arrives in Fetter-Rothnie having undergone a form of nervous breakdown.
For him, the experience of trench warfare has offered a glimpse into an
alternative reality – 'dissolution – a dimension that won't remain stable', a
'fourth dimension', 'off every imaginable plane that the old realities yielded'
(114). This 'fourth dimension' is in many ways similar to the semiotic as
it is described by Kristeva and, like it, offers a challenge to Garry's sense
of identity and the very boundaries of his self. However, while it may be
an aspect of experience uncovered by war, such dissolution is not the basis
on which patriarchy is constructed. Within it, Garry's behaviour can only
be described as a form of mental illness, a temporary aberration. Himself
located within the essentially masculine world of linear time, Garry's longterm response is to move beyond such de-constructing experience to one of
re–construction within the patriarchal spaces of politics, history and social
interaction. In a world 'unmade' by war, Garry seeks to promote what can
be clearly defined: tables, civil engineering, socialism, and a 'definite engagement in the war against evil'(66) in his response to the Louie Morgan
affair. His time in Fetter-Rothnie is thus perplexing, for he is to find that
experience there – just like that he has undergone in the trenches – unsettles,
at least temporarily, his plans for the world and the notions of right and
wrong upon which he has founded them.

However, if Garry is himself troubled by his return to this arena, so too
his arrival also acts as a disruption to the feminine world he finds there :
'[t]he smooth security of seed and egg was gone' the narrator tells us, 'into
this life Garry Forbes came in the second week of April' (48–9). Garry's
presence – and the glimpse of an other, essentially patriarchal world which
he brings with him – serves to rupture the predominantly female world of
the Weatherhouse, bringing it up against the boundaries of alternative, essentially masculine experience and altering the ways in which several of its
inhabitants locate themselves in relation to their surroundings.

Such dislocation, as she is brought up against the boundaries between two apparently conflicting spaces, is the root of much of Lindsay Lorimer's anxiety in the text. The youngest inhabitant of the Weatherhouse, Lindsay shares more than any other character in the novel the 'developmental' role occupied by Martha Ironside of *The Quarry Wood*. Thus at a crucial stage in the formation of her own identity, Lindsay is profoundly affected by her time at Fetter-Rothnie as she confronts the different kinds of experience delineated in the novel.

On her arrival at the Weatherhouse life is reasonably straight-forward for Lindsay. Clear-headed in her love for Garry and his ideals, Lindsay is anxious to insert herself into his world, that of patriarchal Law. It is, Kristeva suggests, by an entry into signifying structures – the world of 'names' and language – that we enter the symbolic order, rupturing a pre-linguistic confluence between self and the other. Consequently, Lindsay's desire to enter this domain may be recognised by her eagerness to name the world she discovers around her. As Ellen suggests that 'names don't matter very much', Lindsay responds:

'Oh, yes. Names – they're like songs.' And she chanted in a singing voice, 'Wild duck, wild duck, kingfisher, curlew. Their names are a part of themselves. Can you tell me where to see a kingfisher, Cousin Ellen?' (47).

For Lindsay this desire to locate herself within the patriarchal, signifying world and to fix what she sees around her by nomenclature is bound up with her love for Garry. 'Seduced' by his talk of politics and war, Lindsay is inspired to share the world he wishes to recreate after his experiences in the trenches: 'He told them all that was to be accomplished to make life worthier. Lindsay glowed. This was the talk she loved to hear' (84).

During her sojourn to the Weatherhouse, however, Lindsay discovers that the countryside is not only 'wonderful' (47) but also problematic, seemingly perplexing the socially constructed world which Garry has outlined for her, letting her glimpse a space beyond that of politics. Understandably, this experience is troubling, forcing Lindsay to reassess her relationship to Garry and her place in his reconstructed future.

Intrinsic to Lindsay's dislocation are those experiences described in the chapter 'The January Christmas Tree', itself an object adrift in time. Here, Lindsay first meets Garry's aunt Bawbie Paterson, a character whose identification with an area of experience beyond that which Lindsay has previously comprehended, profoundly disturbs her sense of self. Bawbie's alignment with an arena beyond the social is inherent in all descriptions of her and in associations of her with both light and fire. Lindsay first perceives her as an 'elemental mass', 'earthen smelling' (27). Bawbie is 'not like a person', more like 'a thing' (27), beyond Lindsay's understanding of human identity. Yet Lindsay is both attracted and repulsed by Bawbie, recognising that her ability to make her feel 'puny in her grasp', to 'unmake' her as Shepherd has suggested the elements may do, also offers a 'strange exhilaration' (27). Bawbie has chosen to live in a space outside the social order, beyond the Law, a position typified by her resistance to the black-out regulations. She has chosen to locate herself at the very boundaries of society, socialising with tramps, breaking the Fetter-Rothnie dress codes, and as she emphatically tells Garry, refusing resolutely to enter into his model for the future, the patriarchal world of politics and war:

> 'I'm a Paterson of Knapperley, my lad, a Paterson of Knapperley can please himself. It's only your common bodies that need your laws and regulations, to be hauden in about. The folk of race have your law within themselves. Ay, ay, I'm a Paterson of Knapperley, but you're Donnie Forbes's grandson and seek to make yourself a politician. But go your ways' (123).

The dislocation which she experiences as she is caught between Bawbie's world and that which Garry has suggested to her is what initially so distresses Lindsay. Garry's model is, she learns, not a wholly adequate one and she is shocked by his insistence on applying it to the case of Louie Morgan. 'Life's so strange. It isn't what you want' (82) she laments, realising that experience is full of shadows and nuances which she has previously failed to see. Constructing her identity in preparation for marriage, Lindsay finds, is complex, her trip to the Weatherhouse providing a window into realms of experience beyond those which she had recognised, and which Garry refuses to acknowledge as a part of domestic experience.

At the Weatherhouse Lindsay is surrounded by many women, and, we could reasonably suppose, she might look to them for models of how to re-position herself within the apparently conflicting spaces which she has discovered. One possible, but problematic, position for woman, Kristeva suggests, is to seek to locate herself in arenas outside of the 'sublimating word' (1986, 144). The traditional roles for women who seek to inhabit those spaces outside of 'paternal legislation', however, are at best, those of eccentric, and at worst, madwoman, and these are, similarly, the roles offered by Shepherd's text for women who live within these domains.

The role of 'eccentric' is clearly an apt description of Bawbie. Her exuberance, her 'strange exhilaration' stem from what seems a conscious choice to live beyond the social law, and it is a position which, Shepherd suggests, has much to offer for those who are brave enough to adopt it. Bawbie, after all, provides a refreshing alternative to the claustrophobic world of the Weatherhouse and its, at times, petty inhabitants. Shepherd, however, also delineates the fate of those who, like Louie Morgan, do not *choose* to live in such border lands but, more problematically, are apparently caught in a tragic arena beyond that of paternal Law; a world where connections back into the signifying structures of the symbolic order seem impossible.

Such a location within this space is ultimately the source of Louie's tragedy and madness. For Garry, Louie is initially simply a moral problem; her act unambiguously 'evil' she is a slander against the 'truth' which he is determined to recover in memory of his friend David Gray. Louie, he thinks, should be taken before the Kirk Session – that all-powerful representative of the paternal Law in Scotland – for 'public accusation and punishment' (89). However, Louie's case cannot unproblematically be resolved within such a simple framework for as even Garry, to his discomposure, recognises, it is an inappropriate sweetmeat for the Fetter-Rothnie gossips. Her tragedy lies in her dis-location from the straightforward morality posed by Garry. Alienated from this world, Louie seeks to construct identity through a series of sham roles, but ultimately positioned outside the social code, she is unable to re-locate herself back into it. 'Do you suppose words ever mean the right thing?' (99–100) she asks Garry, hinting at her location beyond the signifying structures of language. 'That is a morality more involved than I am accustomed to' (101) Garry complains as she explains the rationale behind what she has done, and Louie responds: 'Morality is always involved. Only truth is clear and one. But we never see it. That's why we must live by morality' (101). While Louie's position may seem bizarre – and ultimately gives way to what can only be defined as 'madness' – her tragedy lies in the fact that, given her own location in a domain beyond any which Garry can comprehend, her words have some logic; morality is more complex than he has realised and in a sense it is his own reality – one based on reconstruction rather than the fluidity of the semiotic – which is missing a dimension.

Less extreme a case, but perhaps one to which we are more sympathetic, is that of Ellen Falconer who, like Louie, is dislocated from the symbolic order. She too has been metaphorically, if not literally, 'locked up in a tower', separated from society by an inability to enter its social frameworks. Like Louie too, her plight is one of excessive imagination through which she constructs for herself a space outside the social – a space which merges into the primordial light and darkness beyond her tower like room. Unlike Lindsay, Ellen is incapable of defining the world by nomenclature recognising, rather, a confluence between self and object beyond that of language:

> 'I hardly know their names, Linny'.
> 'But don't you love birds?'
> 'Oh, yes.' Ellen paused, gazing at the eager girl. 'They are a part of myself,' she wanted to say; but how could one explain that? Where it had to be explained it could not be understood. 'You are a part of me, too,' she thought, with her eyes fixed on Lindsay's where she waited for her answer. Her lips were parted and her eyes shone; and Mrs Falconer longed to tell her of the strange secret of life – how all things were one and there was no estrangement except for those who did not understand. But all that she could find to say was, 'I know hardly any of their names' (47).

Like Louie's position, Ellen's is to some extent a valid one, yet, imprisoned within it, she is literally lost for words, and, as a result, alienated from Lindsay and all others whom she seeks to love in the novel. Her strange 'bumming' sets her apart from the world she wishes to inhabit, a symbolic order which she cannot enter.

Ellen's position in this alternative, pre-linguistic arena is one which she cannot escape from, and it is thus, ironically, when she finds her tongue that her tragedy arises. Seeking to act in the 'real' world which Garry has outlined for her (thus offering a tragic counterpoint to Lindsay) Ellen rises with her teeth chattering, speaking with a voice which doesn't 'seem to come from her throat' (156) to denounce Louie. Thus acting in a manner alien to her entire nature, Ellen's attempt to enter Garry's political, patriarchal world is, inevitably, a failed one, and the consequences again a form of 'madness' and early death.

While Bawbie and the abiding image of her dancing a Highland fling for herself in her kitchen may represent the attractions of a choice to live beyond the Law, the fates of Louie and Ellen suggest the pain and madness which results from those 'locked in the tower', trapped within an arena where they can have no access to the symbolic order. There is, these women suggest, a high price to be paid for an inability to locate oneself within the patriarchal domain, a price which Ellen recognises towards the end of the novel when she perceives that her own world of 'imagination' has been, as Kristeva's thesis would support, at the cost of any sense of identity:

> But as she sat miserably by her window she saw all at once that it was not only the bird's name of which she was ignorant: it was the whole world outside herself . . .
> . . . One could not be taken into other lives except by learning what they were in themselves. Ellen had never cared to know. In her imaginings other people had been what she decreed, their real selves she ignored. 'I have despised them all.' She felt miserably small, imprisoned wholly in herself (182).

Such imprisonment and alienation Shepherd suggests, is, if women's natural space is one beyond patriarchal law and language, the tragic fate of femininity. However, her novel also offers other, and more happy possibilities for how the feminine may be located within the apparently contradictory spaces of women's time and linear time, the semiotic and the symbolic.

In his essay on Nan Shepherd, Roderick Watson suggests that her work is essentially about the roles which an intelligent woman can create for herself within the confines of her society:

> All three books deal with attempts to find space for personal priorities within the community circle of traditional values. These pressures are doubly telling in that Nan Shepherd's protagonists are educated young women in the 1920s and the 1930s, who become aware that there must be more for them in life than the role customarily assigned to them by their own class (1990, 208).

Indeed, alongside those driven mad by a failure to position themselves within the 'community circle' and those who choose the eccentricity of living beyond it, Shepherd's novel also offers the example of women who, to greater or lesser degrees, opt to position themselves within some kind of half-way house, negotiating for themselves a complex area between the semiotic and the social.

This is a space adopted by many of the other inhabitants of the Weatherhouse; by Tris and Paradise and by Leeb who, though we are reminded of her unlikely resemblance to Ellen on several occasions, has lived long enough to adopt a kind of ironic detachment to the life she sees around her. For Tris, such pragmatism is encapsulated in a desire to look to another of the perspectives offered by the windows of the Weatherhouse, that of a wider community beyond herself. Her maxim 'a ga'in foot's aye gettin'' (7) offers her a route into this larger perspective, that of news, gossip and community affairs. While such a means of location may, no more than Bawbie's or Ellen's, be ideal, it offers a means of escape from the imprisonment of self, a tortured inability to escape the confines of one's own painful boundaries.

Such a position is essentially a practical one, and, not surprisingly, it is the space adopted by Kate, who shares with her mother the Weatherhouse's many windowed room. Kate, we are told, 'liked making a bed and contriving a dinner'(10), in other words entering into the 'quiet domesticity'(10) of life, a path beyond herself towards others which frees her from an obsession with the darkness that has engulfed her mother. For Kate, life is essentially pragmatic; Lindsay's perplexities, while sympathised with, are 'hysterical'(132) and any passion she may have herself felt for Garry subsumed in the common sense decision that 'lying awake brought scanty profit'(38). This position too, is one shared by the lesser characters in the novel; by Mrs Hunter and Francie's wife Bell. These women position themselves within an essentially patriarchal system but succeed, at least to some degree, in negotiating their own spaces within it; in Bell's case her own bed, in Barbara's her right to the largesse of hospitality. For Shepherd, such a positioning is essentially social; located in a recognition that the life of the community is based upon the willingness of its inhabitants to 'rub along', tolerating the differences within itself. While such positions may not be ideal (in fact they at times seem like compromise) they suggest that looking outside the tower of the Weatherhouse to the perspectives beyond its windows has much to offer.

This is the position which, in the end, is adopted by Lindsay, the third character to inhabit the Weatherhouse's 'elfin' half-way house. No longer frightened of Bawbie, Lindsay reconstructs her sense of identity, marrying Garry and choosing to locate herself within his essentially patriarchal world. For her, the tragedy of Louie Morgan is, just as life is for Leeb, contained within the confines of a charming story – something which can no longer do harm. Her engagement with the 'semiotic' landscape of Fetter-Rothnie is re-absorbed into a social order of marriage and children; they no longer stay with Bawbie when they visit ('we can't stay in the house now. It's unspeakable. She's beyond everything' (194)). Garry similarly reconstitutes himself after his nervous breakdown into the world of politics. He, we are told, frequently speaks at meetings; Lindsay, we might surmise, may be his greatest supporter. By her visit to the Weatherhouse Lindsay has been 'unmade' but, unlike the unfortunate Louie or Ellen, she has also been 'steadied again', reconstituted into an adult self, which, if not without losses, offers one practical method of procedure for a woman.

Lindsay's solution to the problem of location is, however, only one alternative in a novel which does not privilege any single position but suggests rather, that in a world fraught with complexities for female identity, each must negotiate her own response. Lindsay's position offers a possibility, but it is not reified, suggesting no long term promise of happiness:

> Happy – there was no doubt of it. Now who could have foretold that such a marriage would turn out well? . . .
> . . . Well, she might repent it yet. Nine years was not so very long a time . . . (194–5)

Other responses to the problems of location are, this would suggest, equally valid, be they Leeb's, or Ellen's or Kate's, a fact reiterated in the circumstances surrounding Ellen's death. To her family, though grieved sincerely, Ellen's life may seem faintly ridiculous. Yet, somewhat unexpectedly, to Stella Ferguson, she is a 'precious saint', a 'stunner' (203). We are reminded that 'angels of light', as well as 'angels of darkness' (79), may arise in the most unlikely of places.

This open-ended conclusion to the novel is both typical of Shepherd's work and a reminder that a reluctance to privilege any one response to the dilemmas of location within an essentially patriarchal world is at the very foundation of *The Weatherhouse*. While Joy Hendry has suggested that the novel may be 'too diversified'(1987, 305), its diversity is part of its very structure; consciously lacking a protagonist, all characters in the novel offer valid responses to the dilemmas of space and location which it explores. 'Knowing another is endless', writes Shepherd in *The Living Mountain*. To realise this, she concludes, is 'the final grace accorded from the mountain', a 'journey into Being' which is beyond the desires of self and its sharply defined boundaries' (1977; 1996, 94). 'They too are men' (174), Ellen tells Garry as he discovers dark and unfamiliar aspects of community life in Fetter-Rothnie and Shepherd's vision of social interaction is a similarly broad kirk, demanding that all aspects of experience find a space within the canvas of a world so vast that 'it will take a long time to get to the end of' (1977; 1996, 79) it.

The Weatherhouse is, as a result, a novel which *explores* possible locations of the feminine within society, not one which offers any simple models of identity; it is a novel of questions not of solutions. Rather than presenting any one ideal position for women in society (or for men either, for that matter) it examines the difficulties inherent in the very concept of identity, and in locating the self in relation to society. Such a position is likely to be perplexing for those who look for straightforward responses to questions of regional or gender identity in Shepherd's texts, for *The Weatherhouse* is a novel which 'unmakes' the reader's assumptions about his/her position in the world but does not necessarily offer the consolation of steadying us again into new certainties. It is this aspect of her work which makes it an awkward subject for criticism, for such multiplicity does not lend itself easily to reductive analysis. It is notable that *A Pass in the Grampians*, perhaps the most indeterminate of all Shepherd's novels, has been the last to be re-printed in a modern edition. This refusal to locate the feminine in any one fixed position does, however, offer the indeterminacy which critics like Kristeva suggest may be the only possible response of women to the dilemmas of location. 'It is not possible to say of a *woman* what she *is* (without running the risk of abolishing her difference)' writes Kristeva (1986, 161). 'They too are women' Shepherd might have written in a later age, including Bawbie, Louie, Lindsay, Ellen, and the rest of the women in *The Weatherhouse* as aspects of the feminine; responses to the problems of location in an infinitely complex and irreducible world, a world in which concepts of self and identity cannot be fixed but, on the contrary, are invigoratingly unmade.

Works Cited

Craig, Cairns 'Twentieth Century Scottish Literature: An Introduction' in *The History of Scottish Literature*. Cairns Craig ed. vol.4. Aberdeen: Aberdeen University Press, 1987, 1–9

Hendry, Joy 'Twentieth-century Women's Writing: The Nest of Singing Birds' in *The History of Scottish Literature*. vol. 4, 291–309

Hewitt, David 'The North-East: Literature and Identity' in *Northern Visions: Essays on the Literary Identity of Northern Scotland in the Twentieth Century*. David Hewitt ed. East Linton: Tuckwell Press, 1995

Kristeva, Julia *The Kristeva Reader*. Toril Moi ed. Oxford: Basil Blackwell, 1986

Shepherd, Nan *The Grampian Quartet: The Quarry Wood* [1928], *The Weatherhouse* [1930], *A Pass in the Grampians* [1933], *The Living Mountain* [1977]. Edinburgh: Canongate Classics, 1996

Watson, Roderick '. . . to get leave to live: Patterns of Identity, Freedom and Defeat in the Fiction of Nan Shepherd' in *Studies in Scottish Fiction: Twentieth Century*. Joachim Schwend and Horst W. Drescher eds. Frankfurt am Main: Peter Lang, 1990, 207–18

Whyte, Christopher ed. *Gendering the Nation: Studies in Modern Scottish Literature*. Edinburgh: Edinburgh University Press, 1995

Naomi Mitchison (1897–1999)

Naomi Mitchison, born Naomi Haldane in 1897 in Edinburgh, grew up in Oxford where she attended the Dragon School and St Anne's College. Her summers were spent at the family estate at Cloan, Auchterarder, so that she retained a sense of Scottish identity throughout her formative years. In 1915 she became a Voluntary Aid Detachment nurse in London. She married G.R. Mitchison in 1916; they subsequently had seven children, five of whom are still living. G.R. Mitchison (known as Dick) died in 1970. Mitchison's commitment to socialist politics was reflected in trips to Russsia (1932) and Austria (1934). She stood for Parliament as Labour candidate for the Scottish Universities in 1935. Her move to Carradale, on the Mull of Kintyre, in 1937, marked the beginning of a long involvement with Scottish, particularly Highland, social and political issues; from 1945–66 she was a member of Argyll County Council, as well as being a member of the Highland Panel from 1947–64, and the Highlands and Islands Development Council from 1966–1976. From 1963–89 she was Mmarona and tribal adviser to the Bkagatla of Botswana. She died in January 1999.

Mitchison published her first novel *The Conquered* in 1923; this set a precedent for her later works in the genre of the historical novel. Major works include *The Corn King and the Spring Queen* (1931), *The Bull Calves* (1947), *The Blood of the Martyrs* (1948). Mitchison published over twenty novels for adults, a large body of children's fiction, three books of poetry, several plays, collections of short stories, as well as social and political non-fiction. In 1962 *Memoirs of a Spacewoman* marked Mitchison's move into the genre of science fiction. Her autobiographical works include *Small Talk* (1973), *All Change Here* (1975), *You May Well Ask* (1979), and *Among You, Taking Notes 1939–1945* (1985)

M.E.

The Location of Magic in *The Corn King and the Spring Queen*

Margaret Elphinstone

Naomi Mitchison's *The Corn King and the Spring Queen* may seem at first sight to be an unlikely text to choose to embody the impulse of modernism in Scottish women's writing. It can perhaps more easily be placed as a historical novel in the genre established by Scott: that is to say, it is a novel which invites us to consider the individual as a historical being, by showing us the interaction between the individual in society and the dynamic of history. Furthermore, there are clear political parallels between the post-classical world created in the text and the 1930s in which it was written. However, the social/historical theme is mediated through a constant re-negotiation of what is real, as the stability of social, rational and geographical boundaries is undermined by the eruption of magic into realist historical narrative. The element of magic within the social world of the text can be correlated to the psychoanalytic model of the unconscious within the psychic world, which also remains beyond the boundaries of social restraints, and disrupts rational paradigms from within. Through the force of magic, the text subverts unified, external definitions of reality, including a simple moral opposition of good and evil. I argue, therefore, that this is a thoroughly modernist text in so far as it evades fixed definitions apparently rooted in the facts of the external world, and presents meaning from multiple and contradictory perspectives, locating it in a psychic world which will always partially elude rational classification.

The operation of magic in history, within the text, is similar to the operation of fiction on historical narrative; the magic of Erif Der has a self-reflexive quality as it echoes the creation of an imagined reality through writing, valorising narrative over the very concept of external fact. Mitchison's use of her sources becomes in this context highly ironic. Two principal literary sources, acknowledged in her 1990 Introduction to *The Corn King and the Spring Queen* are the *Cambridge Ancient History* (Vol VII, 1928) and Frazer's *The Golden Bough* (1922). Neither of these source texts, of course, overtly acknowledges the magical powers of the individual, or, indeed, the authority of subjectivity at all. However, the magic that is included in the paradigm of the fictional text subverts the apparently rational objectivity of the historical and scientific account. For example, the plot and characters of the Spartan narrative in *The Corn King and the Spring Queen* are all there in the *Cambridge Ancient History* (Vol VII, 752–762). The story of Cleomenes, in the history, is glossed with a judgement that Cleomenes 'made his pathetic decision that death was too easy', and the narrative ends with the comment: 'History must regret that Cleomenes had not died with his Spartans at Sellasia' (*CAH*, 762). 'History' here not only has a specific, individual point of view, but it also regrets the failure of the king to enact a literally pre-scribed, ahistorical myth. For the authors of *The Cambridge Ancient History*, as for Mitchison, the rational, conscious and historic is not, when one reads between the lines, absolutely aloof from the felt, unconscious and mythic. Mitchison's novel, in effect, reveals the implicit subject position in the historical narrative and makes a revision in which this subtext becomes explicit.

The most obvious difference between *The Golden Bough* and *The Corn King and the Spring Queen* is, as with *The Cambridge Ancient History*, that of genre, and the authority that genre assumes. Mitchison's debt to Frazer in terms of details of rituals concerning the Corn Year and the ritual death of the King is clear. What is perhaps less obvious is her revision of Frazer's text in terms of point of view. There is a significant echo from one text to the other when Hyperides the Epicurean is commenting on the rituals of Marob, and says:

'Timokrates, have I done well? Have I followed Epicuros, our master, who first understood that science, showing the laws of nature, also showed a unity and harmony beyond all superstition and all the horrors and follies which men have made for themselves?' (410)

Frazer ends his scientific enquiry into magic and religion in similar terms:

. . . we may well ask ourselves whether there is not some more general conclusion, some lesson if possible, of hope and encouragement, to be drawn from the melancholy record of human error and folly which has engaged our attention in this book (1922; 1967, 930).

Hyperides the character, like Frazer the author, studies the myth exhaustively with obvious fascination, and yet ultimately distances himself from personal implication by an assertion of scientific objectivity and truth. The disruption of the rational world by an unruly unconscious or a savage myth, is, in spite of the fact that both of these may be subject matter for scientific enquiry, something that both the fictional and the actual writer disown. And yet, the scientist, like the historian, belies his objectivity within his own text. In *The Corn King and the Spring Queen*, Erif's magic and Sphaeros' scientific rationality are both ways of representing reality. Erif and Sphaeros are equally implicated in events, and both provide perspectives from which to assess what transpires. Mitchison's revision of Frazer's text puts the apparently detached, rational observer back into the flux of nature and history. There is no outside, omniscient point of view; everyone is a part of the myth, and the authoritative voice has become a character inside the text.

Mitchison not only revises Frazer's text, she also draws upon Freud's psychoanalytic model, an intertextual combination that has been well documented in several major modernist texts[1]. The irony of Frazer's repudiation of Freud's work has also been discussed elsewhere [2]. Mitchison's text compounds that irony by explicitly closing the gap between narrative point of view and its subject in Frazer's text, in her fictional revision. She does this in many ways; the scope of the novel is vast, so in this essay I shall concentrate on the magical powers of the two eponymous characters who are the primary focus of the novel. In this context the magic of Marob would seem to relate to the element described in Freud's essay *Das Unheimlich* (1919), in which he discusses 'the uncanny' as one aspect of the eruption of the unconscious into the heart of civilisation:

This uncanny is in reality nothing new or alien, but something which is familiar and old–established in the mind and which had become alienated from it only through the process of repression (363–4).

Erif's magic seems to come from the same place, and indeed, in *Das Unheimlich*, Freud mentions 'animism, magic and sorcery' as three of the factors which 'turn something frightening into something uncanny'. Marob magic does not fit in with paradigms of reason or probability, and yet it seems recognisable, in Freudian terms, as an aspect of the unconscious.

What is frightening about it is precisely the fact that it seems familiar. Erif's journey into a historical world takes her to a place (literally and meta-phorically) where for the first time she is called upon to *explain* her magic. Perhaps that is when it first becomes an art; as a representation it can now be seen from the outside as well as being part of experienced life. Erif's role in the novel subverts the rational principles of science and philosophy, represented within the text by Stoicism. Magic valorises the significance of what the subject perceives, and the power of individual ritual, over an idea of objective reality or logical response to it.

The novel opens with Erif Der, who seems familiar although her time is alien, as we first find her throwing stones into the Black Sea, an action which is both ordinary and primeval in its connotations. One might contrast this image of Erif with the later introduction to Phylilla in the world of Sparta: Phylilla is shooting arrows at a target as she prepares to be a true Spartan warrior, a ploy which is neither familiar to the reader, nor does it spring from any deeply-felt source of shared images. Phylilla remains distant, an archaic figure living in a world whose rationale we do not share. Erif and Marob are first presented in terms of the childlike and the primeval, both of which are familiar to us in terms of an experience shaped by literary and psychoanalytical constructions.

It is in this context that we discover almost at once that Erif can work magic. She magics Yersha into not seeing her pass (4), and then she magics Berris into taking off all his clothes in the middle of the street (8). Her own power is for her a part of the natural world. However, we then realise that we are meeting her at the point when this innocent state is reaching its end. When Erif faces her father, we see that she is aware of her identity as sepa-rate, not part of the natural order or even of he family. Harn Der asks her: 'What are you afraid of?' and she replies: 'Myself. My own power' (5). A little later this is amplified: 'She knew her magic depended on her self and could be as much broken as she was' (19). Erif's magic, which is part of the women's magic of Marob, is both ordinary and primeval. Moreover, as Marob moves from a primeval to a historical world, so the main char-acters, Erif, Berris and Tarrick, move from an experience of oneness with their world to a state of dislocation, and their quest in life then becomes either the search for healing, or for perfection in art.

The arrival of Sphaeros, the Stoic philosopher, causes a major disruption in the cyclical world of Marob. However, Marob up until that point is not the complete opposite to all that Sphaeros represents. There has already been contact with Greece. Tarrick/Charmantides, and other characters, are already divided selves with two names. Tarrick and Yersha have been in

Hellas; Tarrick already has 'the Greek part of himself'. Epigethes has already caused Berris to distance himself from his own art, so for him art can never again be naive and spontaneous expression, he must always be critic as well as artist, questioning form and appearance even while he creates it. When Sphaeros first arrives, a pattern forms in which he and Erif become opposites between which other characters move, although, like all oppositions in the novel, this one is set up only to be dissolved again into further reflecting images. Erif's initiation into the adult world has already been presented as a journey into separation. She is already torn by conflicting loyalties, already questioning her own identity. She is not simply the barbarian woman in contrast to the Hellenic man.

Erif recognises that Sphaeros does not respond to her magic after the shipwreck: 'I can't', said Erif Der suddenly, 'I can't! It doesn't work on him!' (60). When Erif and Sphaeros struggle for ascendancy over Tarrick at the bullfight, magic and philosophy come into direct conflict, and yet, even here, the polarity between two appearances is undermined at the moment of conflict. Sphaeros saves Tarrick from Erif's spell, but not merely through an idea, although his success with Tarrick is to 'Make him think' (73), but also through an intervention in which all the emphasis is on the physical body: '. . . so that for one moment she saw only the hard jut of muscles in his arm and shoulder, wondered dizzily at a middle-aged philosopher being like that . . .' (73). A moment later Sphaeros is physically injured, and as Tarrick says, 'You risked your life to save me' (75).

Sphaeros is never the abstract embodiment of a philosophy. He is a man with a body and emotions. When he is an old man in Egypt, suffering the death of all those whom in spite of his philosophy he loves, he has become more, not less, connected to the experienced world from which it was his life's purpose to abstract himself. Stoicism informs the novel, and its doctrines are mainly expounded through Sphaeros. However, representations of Stoicism are never unilateral. Sphaeros is unable to recognise that Erif's magic is also part of the divine order of things; he sees her activities as somehow outside his cosmos: '. . . he had a certain prejudice against Erif Der; she was the kind of person who disturbed life and made it run against its natural and divine order' (178).

So there are aspects to life which Sphaeros deliberately leaves out, failing perhaps to see that they are actually another manifestation of the way of nature that he asserts. Erif's magic is certainly a disruptive force, but it is less alien than Sphaeros thinks. Just as Marob finds reflections in the heart of Sparta, in the helot festivals, so too Erif's magic exists at the very heart of what appears to Sphaeros to be its opposite, in the psyche of the civilised Greek.

The language of Stoicism appears on almost every page of *The Corn King and the Spring Queen*. When Sphaeros is half conscious after the bullfight: '"Truth" he said clearly, in Greek, truth is – a fire – God – Charmantides, my truth –"' (75). Fire, in Stoic philosophy, is the dynamic principle that infuses creation. But Erif Der's name is also fire, although it is hidden in a simple reversal. (Moreover, it is a reversal in English, so it invites the reader to make a connection that exists entirely outside the imaginary language of the fictional world, which is to say, outside Sphaeros' frame of reference). Erif's magic raises two issues, which are also the primary concerns of Stoicism. The first is a moral issue. Sphaeros asserts the Stoic position that the most important thing is to know how to live, because if one knows what is good one cannot help but do it. The second issue follows from the first: if goodness requires knowledge, then it becomes crucial to understand how one relates to the universe. Moral purpose must begin with grasping at reality in the moment that it becomes apparent, the process described as *kataleptike phantasia*. Erif's magic, Tarrick's kingship, and Berris' art, grapple with precisely these issues: all three characters continually raise questions about what is good, and what is real, and for all three their morality derives directly from their perception of truth.

Perhaps Sphaeros' initial failure to include Erif in his scheme of things is the inevitable failure of any perspective to be absolute. The reality that the Marob characters reflect back to Stoicism actually undermines, as well as confirms, its basic principles. As Hyperides later acknowledges, it includes things which philosophy leaves out. Goodness is therefore based not just on different premises, but on something quite different from philosophic premise in the first place. Marob precludes debate or dialectic. It forbids perception or goodness to be reduced to principles of logic, and therefore it dislocates the whole rational paradigm.

Tarrick, who is also Charmantides, is both Corn King of Marob and part Greek. He is only freed from Erif's magic and Harn Der's plot because Sphaeros can 'make him think', and yet he is far from repudiating the magic world. When he and Erif are on their way home from Sparta, they have this exchange:

(Erif:) ' . . . what I was doing then wasn't quite magic. It was more real, I think, not an appearance.'

Tarrick said: 'Your magic is not an appearance, Erif. You are not to say it is.'

... 'Why not?'

'Because I don't want to hear any more about appearance and reality. Because I've left Greece and I am going to be King of my own country' (200).

For the Corn King the magic of Marob must be real. Only then can he be sure of his own godhead, in which role he can without taking thought be both immortal and right. Sphaeros' gift of abstract thought is a backhanded one, in that Tarrick's knowledge of his own separateness confers upon him both mortality and a conscience. The passage from god to man parallels in many ways the dislocation of the conscious from the unconscious self in Freudian analysis and the induction into language in Lacan's post-Freudian paradigm. When Tarrick returns to Marob for the first time he took 'a great deal of thought about how to be king' (206), but this rational, self-conscious approach to a role that has previously been natural to him soon fails him. Mitchison is never sentimental about the savagery of Marob. From the beginning we have seen the barbaric aspect of the Corn King, for example in the killing of Epigethes, but Tarrick's orgy of torture and brutality after he returns from Greece is more disturbing (230, 232). The uncontrollable regression of an apparently civilised man seems to be an inevitable reaction to the Stoic demand that the individual be governed by pure reason. Sphaeros has made Tarrick aware of himself as a separate, thinking, individual, but his philosophy has nothing to offer when what follows inevitably is Tarrick's confrontation with the fact of his own mortality:

He used not to mind, used not to think of himself as anything apart from Marob, which went on forever. It was the Greek part of him standing up in his heart and whispering. The Corn King would always be there, but Tarrick only for a few more years (216).

Later he tells Erif, 'I am tired of playing the game for the corn, making it go on ... but leaving myself out' (221). Not only must Tarrick face the fact of death, but he has also acquired the necessary distance from himself to judge his actions in terms of right and wrong:

Why could not the Corn King do as he chose! Then he began to reason about it, to follow this queer process which Sphaeros had taught him,

the thing the Greeks used instead of magic. He discovered that it was
Sphaeros who had put this thing into him, who had even given him
the words for good and evil: this sort of good and evil which were to
do with him, Tarrick-Charmantides, and nothing to do with the Corn
King of Marob, whose only good was the good of the Corn (232).

There is no going back for Tarrick; only at the rituals when he is all Corn
King can he 'drop this painful, too-conscious self' (250). At other times
he wrestles with the books that Sphaeros has left, hating them because the
very process of writing has made the ideas seem alien and dead to him,
and because they emphasise the fact that he is 'out of harmony', dislocated
from the old life that had satisfied all the Corn Kings before him (252-3).
    Tarrick finds healing at last when he and Hyperides are prisoners of
the Red Riders. In explaining himself to Hyperides the Greek Epicurean, it
seems as if Tarrick at last comes to terms with himself as both individual
and Corn King. The irony is that his apotheosis is narrated by Hyperides,
the Greek who begins by describing Tarrick as 'a big, lazy-looking, smiling
savage' (405), and who recognises in Marob something very like Freud's
'unheimlich':

'. . . there's a queer feeling about this town. I don't know quite what
makes it, but I keep on suddenly finding myself at grips with the most
horrible, undefined fear, the sort of thing I thought I had grown out
of long ago and would never feel again. I repeat to myself that it is
quite baseless and that fear of the unknown is a shameful thing for a
reasonable, scientific-minded person to have in his head . . . ' (406).

Hyperides' narrative is ironic because it initially pre-supposes a vast difference between himself and Tarrick, but the subtext of his story is that the
two men mirror one another, with significant differences. Hyperides points
out the irony of Tarrick's explanation of his role as Corn King as 'the way
of Nature': a Stoic phrase. Tarrick can only explain what he is in the language of separation; he never had to find words for what he was until he
has partly ceased to be it. Hyperides describes his new understanding of
Tarrick's predicament as an act of 'imaginative goodwill': 'I can get into his
mind '(416). But the process is not one way; Hyperides has been responding
to Tarrick and Marob too, recognising in it from the first something which
is frightening because it is familiar. He is able at the end of his imprisonment
with Tarrick to conclude, 'There is no such thing as an individual. We are
not divided one from another, friend from friend' (418).

As in *The Golden Bough*, there are many god kings besides Tarrick in *The Corn King and the Spring Queen*: each story that we are told reflects other stories in other places. Kleomenes not only deliberately looks back to Agis, but he unconsciously reflects the stance of the statue of Apollo as he stands beneath it (161). Tarrick, as one embodiment of the king who dies, is also surrounded by reflections of himself. The 'IT', or scapegoat, of the Corn Play is one other manifestation of his role, who ritually dies in his stead. Both Kleomenes and Tarrick change the role of King as well as re-enact it, and this is where the revision of the Christian story becomes consciously ironic in a way that Frazer, in spite of the implications of *The Golden Bough*, overtly evades. When Erif, for personal reasons, brings in Death to the ritual of the Corn Year, Tarrick saves the Year by an unprecedented resurrection: 'He was not Tarrick any more, he was one raised from the dead in the sight of the people' (262–3).

It is the intrusion of personal motivation, which manifests itself in an unprecedented, that is, historic, event, that makes Erif and Tarrick unlike any previous Corn King and Spring Queen:

(Erif:) 'Surely other men and women have found that they could not always be gods!'

Tarrick said: 'They have never thought about it before because it has never happened. We two are different from any Corn King and Spring Queen that Marob has ever had ' (284).

However, it is as individuals that Tarrick and Erif change the endless ritual and bring new insight and healing. At the end of the novel Tarrick has gone, but there is still a Corn King. Erif Gold the daughter of Essro and Berris makes her magic through art, and Tisamenos the defeated Spartan finds his personal liberation in Marob. Through individual action and consciousness some kind of resolution has been reached that goes beyond the personal and into history.

Many characters in *The Corn King and the Spring Queen* embody this painful birth of individual consciousness out of the timelessness of myth. There are moments when one character or another seems to grasp something which to them is real, a moment of apprehension which corresponds to the stoic *kataleptike phantasia*, but these moments occur only within the consciousness of an individual. In the face of the disruptive element of magic, no universal principle, either as explanation of the natural world or as guideline for human behaviour, can be valorised. Thus the text itself, which has made magic central to its fictional world, also locates meaning in the multiple and contradictory impressions of the psyche. Just as the unified authority of the Christian myth is endlessly deferred in the reflecting images of the kings who die, so too the rational principles of Sphaeros are finally located in his own subjectivity.

I began by suggesting that *The Corn King and the Spring Queen* is a modernist text because it locates meaning in individual perception and imagination, that is to say, in the psyche. Furthermore, the text uses magic as a metaphor for the non-rational workings of the unconscious, which as part of the psyche is also a part of meaning. The intertextual relationship between the novel and texts like *The Cambridge Ancient History* and *The Golden Bough* is one in which the relationship between apparent fact and overt fiction, therefore, becomes highly ironic. The magic of *The Corn King and the Spring Queen* is the source of power, not only for witchcraft and kingship but also of all narrative authority. The narrator, like Erif, has the power to imitate nature by sympathetic magic, creating figments of the imagination that reflect life as she sees it and makes others see it. By extension, all narrators have this uncanny power, however much they, and the genre they write in, protest authorial objectivity. The magic of *The Corn King and the Spring Queen*, by subverting rational, objective paradigms of an external world, relocates authority of all kinds in the world of subjective perception and the uncanny images that dwell in the psychic unconscious.

Notes

1. See, for example, J. Vickery.
2. See, for example, Downie, chap.1.

Works Cited

Cook, S. A., F. E. Adcock, M. P. Charlesworth eds. *The Cambridge Ancient History: Volume VII: The Hellenistic Monarchies and the Rise of Rome*. Cambridge: Cambridge University Press, 1928

Downie, R. A. *Frazer and the Golden Bough*. London: Gollancz, 1970

Frazer, J. G. *The Golden Bough: A Study in Magic and Religion.* 1922;
   London: Macmillan, 1967
Freud, Sigmund 'Das Unheimlich' in *Freud 14. Art and Literature.* 1919;
   London: Pelican, 1985
Mitchison, Naomi *The Corn King and the Spring Queen.* 1931; Edinburgh:
   Canongate, 1990
Sandbach, F. H. *The Stoics.* London: Chatto and Windus, 1975
Vickery, J. *The Literary Impact of the Golden Bough.* Princeton, New Jersey:
   Princeton University Press, 1973

Willa Muir (1890–1970)

Willa Muir, born Wilhelmina Anderson, 1890, in Montrose to Shetland parents; educated Montrose Academy and University of St Andrews where she took a first class degree in classics, 1911, followed by a further year's study with the Berry Scholarship, 1911–12; she had a one year assistantship in the classics department, St. Andrews University, 1914–15, then taught Latin and educational psychology at Gypsy Hill Training College, London. She met Edwin Muir in Glasgow, 1918, and married him, 1919. They lived in London till 1921, then in Prague, Germany, Italy, Montrose, and France, 1921–26; they lived mainly in England, 1927–35. They translated works from German, such as Lion Feuchtwangler's *Jew Süss* (1926) and Franz Kafka's *The Trial* (1937) to finance themselves. In *Belonging* (1968), Muir's memoir of Edwin which also acts as her autobiography, she indicates that sometimes most of the translation was done by her, at other times they split it in half. She also translated alone under the name Agnes Neill Scott. *Women: An Inquiry* was published by Hogarth Press, 1925, much of it discussing ideas, now outdated, of essentialised male/female differences. She wrote *Imagined Corners* (1931) between 1926 and 1931 and continued translating for money. Her son Gavin was born in 1927. *Mrs Ritchie*, her second novel, was published in 1933. *Mrs Grundy in Scotland* (1936) was written for a series of works on Scotland devised by Lewis Grassic Gibbon. Muir continued her own writing, mainly short pieces, including radio talks, doggerel verse, and her journals, but also wrote two unpublished novels, *Mrs Muttoe and the Top Storey*, completed 1940, and *The Usurpers*, 1951–52. The Muirs lived in St Andrews, 1935–42, Edinburgh, 1942–45; after the war they lived in both Prague, 1945–49, and Rome, 1949–50. They lived at Newbattle Abbey, Dalkeith, where Edwin was warden 1950–55. After 1955, they mainly lived in Cambridgeshire. Edwin died 1959. Willa took up his contract for a book on the ballads, writing most of it herself: *Living with Ballads* (1965). She lived mainly in London from 1963 and died in Dunoon in 1970.

A.C.

Dreaming Realities: Willa Muir's *Imagined Corners*

Aileen Christianson

Imagined Corners, the title of Willa Muir's first novel, refers to Donne's 'Holy Sonnet' 7:

> At the round earth's imagined corners, blow
> Your trumpets, angels; and arise, arise
> From death, you numberless infinities
> Of souls, and to your scattered bodies go.

Donne's 'round earth's imagined corners' in turn refers to Revelation's 'I saw four angels standing on the four corners of the earth' (7.1) and to judgement day, when 'numberless infinities of souls' and 'scattered bodies' will be brought together. Donne's poem provides a metaphoric framework for the novel, allowing Muir's title to suggest the ways in which her fictional world is bounded by real and imaginary corners. The novel itself combines the imaginary worlds of the unconscious and dreams with the social constructions and ideological framework of Calderwick, the community in which it is set. To encompass all of this, Muir adopts a fluid and multi-voiced narrative style.

As if to counteract the imaginative mystery of the title, Book One of the novel is called 'Calderwick, 1912'; and the opening paragraphs provide a satirical description of the 'burgh of Calderwick'. However, the opening lines, 'that obliquity of the earth with reference to the sun', and the 'arguable uncertainty of the sun's gradual approach and withdrawal in these regions' (1) ensure that the burgh, Scotland, and the novel are all included within a universe where the sun is in uncertain relation to the earth, and the solidity of the town is contrasted with a flow and lack of boundaries in nature, where the larks, crows and gulls do not 'even know they were domiciled in Scotland'(2). By naming Book One 'Calderwick, 1912', Muir separates it from Books Two and Three, 'A Glass is Shaken' and 'Precipitation', grounding it in the pre-war town of Calderwick on the north east coast of Scotland. But she connects the three by introducing on the second page the metaphors of a glass being shaken (water contained) and of precipitation (water natural and uncontrolled).

Human life is so intricate in its relationships that newcomers, whether native or not, cannot be dropped into a town like glass balls into plain water; there are too many elements already suspended in the liquid, and newcomers are at least partly soluble. What they may precipitate remains to be seen (2).

The life of the town is contained like a scientific experiment within a beaker, the rational detached tones of the narrator introducing the metaphor of change, observable but unpredictable. From the perspective of the novel's publication date, 1931, the title of Book One, 'Calderwick, 1912', carried the inevitable reminder that an apparently static world was shortly to be changed unimaginably by World War One.

Muir was later to criticise *Imagined Corners* as having 'enough material in it for two novels, which I was too amateurish to see at the time' (*Belonging*, 163). She was partly referring to its concentration on the interlocking stories of two clearly differentiated family groups, the Shand family: John and Mabel, Elise (Lizzie in her youth), Hector and Elizabeth, and Aunt Janet, and the Murray family: William, the United Free Church minister, Sarah, the unmarried, housekeeping sister, and their brother Ned, paranoid and unsettling, the failed University student. The Murray family are firmly within the post-Kailyard tradition with a leaning to tragedy: there are no solutions other than death, madness and dependence on charity. The Shands on the other hand provide for an exploration of growth and change as well as exploration of socially constructed roles of women and men, and of sexuality through Hector, Elizabeth and Elise. A novel concentrating solely on the Murrays would have referred back to the harsh world of George Douglas Brown's *The House with Green Shutters*. One dealing with the Shand family would have allowed a more modern exploration of gender and sexuality, linking it with Catherine Carswell's *Open the Door!* (1920) and D.H. Lawrence's novels. But by intertwining the two different kinds of novel through a process of doubling and pairing, Elizabeth with

William, Sarah with John, Ned with Elizabeth and Hector, Hector with Elise, Elizabeth with Elise, Muir ensures that the Murrays' lives provide a dark undertow to the Shands', showing that any narratives of growth and change also contain the potential for unfulfilled lives, madness and death, widening the novel's scope beyond the limitations of either tradition.

The narrative format of *Imagined Corners* allows for the intersection of both the inner and outer life of the society of Calderwick. The outer is examined through the exposure of the social forms of the town and an exploration of gender roles and their implicit oppressions imposed on the characters by the society of the time. The inner life is exemplified in the way the narrative point of view throughout the novel moves through the various characters' thoughts, the reader being drawn into an awareness of each character's thought process in turn. Over-identification with any one character is prevented. The inner life is also represented in the ongoing internal analyses by Elizabeth and Elise of their respective psychologies, and in the attention Muir gives to the dreams of her characters. For Muir, dreams represented a reality as strong as any in the conscious world, and she explores this 'dreaming reality' in the novel: 'nobody has seen that the dreams I give my characters are meant to be at least as important as their waking actions' (Pick, 1987, ix). She is intent on probing the psychological depths of the individual, exploring the manner in which all individuals are not 'individual' but products of the ideology of their time and of their particular society. These are the 'countless disconnected existences, bound to their environment'(148) that Elise imagines on her train journey through France from her position of 'peculiar . . . almost god-like detachment from the lives through which she flashes' (148). To ensure the complicated dual process of inner and outer life, Muir creates a structure with 'enough material for two novels in it'. This ensures there is no one consistently central focus for our attention, and that interpretation and response must shift and move along with the narrative.

The use of these methods of narration allows a combination of the 'realist' traditions of the nineteenth and early twentieth century novelists with the newer internalised writing of modernism, of Joyce and the looking within that Woolf had advocated in 'Modern Fiction' (1925; 1994, 4:160). Muir chooses an observant narrator with characteristics shared by the psychoanalyst, the anthropologist, and the scientist: a standing back to assess the culture and the characters, the dissecting, examining and enlarging as through a microscope, the analysis of unexpected conjunctions. Muir was in St. Andrews when J. G. Frazer gave the Gifford Lectures in 1911 and may well have attended them. His articles on 'Taboo' and 'Totemism' had appeared in the ninth edition of *Encyclopedia Britannica* (1875–89) and his ground-breaking work, *The Golden Bough*, was published between 1890 and 1915; Freud drew on his ideas in *Totem and Taboo* (1912–13, trans. 1919), and T.S. Eliot, the critic and poet central to modernism, had acknowledged *The Golden Bough* in his notes to 'The Waste Land' as a 'work of anthropology . . . which has influenced our generation profoundly' (1922). Muir places an armchair anthropologist, Frazer's 'dispassionate observer' (*The Golden Bough* 56), in the novel in Karl, Elise's recently dead husband; he had 'looked at facts as if they were hieroglyphs', and had left behind him seven books, written 'in his study surrounded by mountains of reference–books, without once visiting the countries whose ciphers he unriddled . . . . Karl should have written a book about the primitive people of Scotland . . . . He would have inspected their mythology as if they were Tlinkit Indians. He would have explained their ideology to them. Ideology was a favourite word of his' (149–50). Instead it is his widow Elise who comes to examine her past and her town, to synthesise her earlier rebellious self with her later European self. Muir's narrator, too, can be read as a social anthropologist, assessing the taboos and structures of Calderwick and its inhabitants as Frazer had assessed and compared the magic and religious ritual of primitive societies in *The Golden Bough*. The narrator provides the cold eye of Frazer's 'dispassionate observer' (56), whose voice interprets and analyses throughout the novel. The approach to systems of beliefs, customs and narratives used by anthropologists thus provides Muir with the method for studying the conflicting narratives of the characters and the interwoven beliefs and customs that entrap them, the 'ideology' of the place.

Freud and Frazer are implicitly present when the narrator refers to Elizabeth's 'half–conscious taboos of her youth' (222) and when Elise wants to tell Elizabeth about 'the possible symbolic meaning'(246) of her maid Madeleine's fear of snakes, that she had earlier described to her brother and sister-in-law:

> 'She's full of queer superstitions about animals, almost all of them about the peculiar dangers women run. She thinks that men haven't nearly as much to fear. It must be a very old belief, as old as the affinity between Eve and the serpent; but it's not a belief in companionship; it's a sexual fear of some kind, perhaps'(159).

The wideranging, cross-disciplinary intellectual curiosity of Willa Muir and her contemporaries in the early twentieth century is illustrated by Edwin

Muir, in *An Autobiography* with his description of early discussions with friends in Glasgow (before meeting Willa in 1918), and of his interest in Freud and Jung:

> We . . . discussed everything under the sun: biology, anthropology, history, sex, comparative religion, even theology . . . . We followed the literary and intellectual development of the time, discovering such writers as Bergson, Sorel, Havelock Ellis, Galsworthy, Conrad, E.M.Forster, Joyce, and Lawrence, the last two being contributed by me, for I had seen them mentioned in *The New Age* by Ezra Pound (116). For some years *The New Age* [for which Edwin was to work] had been publishing articles on psychoanalysis, in which Freud and Jung's theories were discussed from every angle, philosophical, religious, and literary, as well as scientific. The conception of the unconscious seemed to throw new light on every human problem and change its terms, and . . . I . . . snatched at it as the revelation which was to transform the whole world of perception (150).

Willa Muir's account in *Belonging* refers to 1933 but applies equally to their earlier years in London, 'Our thoughts and feelings reached out into the cosmos and into the unconscious with a sense of natural freedom, and the whole world of books was ours' (1968, 170).

She explores this 'reaching out' into the unconscious in her characters' dreams in *Imagined Corners*. Frazer had written that 'we seem to move on a thin crust which may at any moment be rent by the subterranean forces slumbering below', meaning the 'solid layer of savagery beneath the surface of society' (1922, 56). Muir uses the same volcanic image to express Elizabeth's fragile control of thought over feeling: 'her thoughts congealed like a crust over her feelings . . . . In another moment her emotions would break their crust and come bubbling up' (115). This metaphor for the uncivilised and for emotion, each pressing uncontrollably on the thin crust of surface civilisation or social control, becomes in Freudian terms the unconscious and the subterranean feelings which surface in dreams. When John Shand has written to ask Elise to visit, after not having communicated with her in twenty years, 'Something hidden very deep seemed to have come alive again' (37); earlier he had 'drifted into sleep with the vague idea that he was stumbling through a dark forest of lofty trees, pursuing a brilliant butterfly that would dart off at a tangent and not keep to the path' (26), his hidden feelings for the sister (rejected because she ran off with a married foreigner), suppressed for twenty years, being expressed in his dream, with its 'dark forest of lofty trees' (26) of tangled sexuality and the uncatchable, unpredictable butterfly. Though Muir does not explore explicitly any sexual feelings John may have had for his sister, it is made clear that she was and is the emotional centre of his life in a way that his wife Mabel, married to him for his social position, cannot be.

Sarah, William Murray's oppressed and unhappy sister, has a dream equally emblematic of her psyche, at a time when she is exhausted by her brother Ned's madness. In an example of narrative analysis early in the novel, Sarah's and Mabel's opposite senses of themselves had been typified through the image of a web:

> Sarah, if she had pictured a web of the world, might have regarded herself as one of many flies caught in it by God, her sole consolation being the presence of the other flies and the impartial symmetry of the web, but Mabel lived at the heart of her own spider's web, and every thread from the outside world led directly to herself (8–9).

Later, as Sarah approaches defeat with Ned, her unconscious refuses the 'impartial symmetry of the web': 'Confused dreams ensnared her; the more she swept out corners the thicker she became entangled in cobwebs, and finally an enormous, hairy spider crawled over her shrinking body' (177). The impartial symmetry of God's purpose has been undermined, and exhaustion and despair have entangled Sarah's unconscious in a threatening web. As well as exemplifying Sarah's supposed lack of access (as a spinster) to sexual feelings, the dream also presages her failure to save her brother Ned and the collapse of her whole system of being, her loss of her place in society. Ned himself is not represented through his dreams; his breakdown forces him to live his unconscious paranoia and madness, not dream it. He lives with his unconscious fears exposed, in a world off-centre to everyone elses'. We see Ned from the outside, through other people's reactions, his inner life invisible and apparently as mysterious and uncontrollable to himself as it is to his sister, even though it can have 'a glimmering of reasonableness in it' (29). His role is to live out the collective fears of the other 'saner' members of his circle, providing unsettling evidence of the precariousness of the mind and the fragility of the human spirit.

Sarah is one of the first characters to appear in the novel and Muir uses her to explore the lack of options for older unmarried women, and the social negativity of their positions: 'If a celestial journalist had asked her what kind of a woman she was she would have replied, with some surprise, that she was a minister's sister' (2–3). This both represents Sarah's own attitude and the social reality of her position; once her brother William has drowned, she has no right to a home in the manse and only a resented charitable action provides her with a place to live. From early in the novel Sarah and William Murray are shown as trapped in the gendered ideology of their time. When 'the exertion of lifting [a] tray was almost too much for' Sarah, it does not occur to her that

> William, being stronger and less tired, might carry the tray into the kitchen. Nor did it occur to William. He had not quite escaped the influence of his father who had ruled his house, as he had ruled his school, on the assumption that the female sex was devised by God for the lower grades of work and knowledge, and that it was beneath the dignity of man to stoop to female tasks. But although this assumption lay at the back of William's mind it appeared so natural that he never recognised it; if Sarah had asked him to carry the tray he would have done so willingly; the assumption merely hindered him from thinking of such an action (16).

This assumption of male superiority, 'devised by God', so internalised that it 'appears . . . natural', is unrecognised by William or Sarah.

Mary and Ann Watson, sisters who are locked together in hatred and dependency, in a sibling relationship that mimics marriage in their differentiated roles of breadwinner and housekeeper, are also shown as being trapped. After Ann locks Mary out of their shared house because it 'belonged' to her, as the shop 'belonged' to Mary, their minister, William Murray, attempting to persuade 'one bitter old woman to give shelter to another', reacts to the threatening appearance of the house; the kitchen window seemed to him 'a dim and evil eye; the cottage was, like himself, a body full of darkness' (101). To William it is like his own spiritual struggle with the concept of evil; but it is also the embodiment of the two sisters' imprisonment. The cottage's 'body full of darkness' seems emblematic of those 'dark places of psychology' that Woolf saw as the concern of modern novelists (1925, 1994, 4:162). Mary Watson had inherited her shop from her father but not his eldership of St. James's United Free Church, 'which was perhaps the reason why her moral vigilance, unremitting in general, was especially relentless towards the minister and elders of that church' (11). Muir makes it clear that these women who think all control must come through 'moral vigilance' are suffering from the gender assumptions of their time: that men, however useless, had the automatic right to positions of power, and that women had access only to the manipulation of men, rather than their own public right to action. Sarah defines this resentfully after Ned's final breakdown: 'If it wasn't for the women the world would be in a gey queer state. And the women get little credit for it' (202); these women are passive victims caught in the web of society. Muir theorises this directly in *Belonging*:

> Male dominance had been my mother's creed and as a child I met it like a toad meeting the teeth of a harrow . . . . The patriarchal Law rated us as second-class citizens (we could not vote) and the patriarchal Church assumed that we were second-class souls (being suspect daughters of that Original Sinner, Eve, we had to cover our heads in church and could not hold ecclesiastical office). There was now no 'parity of esteem' as between male and female in patriarchal structures, whatever values they may have started with . . . . By the time I went to teach in England I was already alert to the comedy of my position as a women in a patriarchally-minded country (1968, 140–41).

But in *Imagined Corners*, Muir expresses the 'comedy' of women's position as a tragedy for women like Sarah, the Watsons and Aunt Janet of the Shand family, with whom an ungrateful Sarah ends up living. They are narrow, limited, and without futures, condemned to insecure and socially rigid lives, unable to imagine escape or enact social change through their own actions, journeying 'from one infinity to another in such a narrow cage' (20), as William thinks of Ann.

Elizabeth, the young, newly married wife of Hector, is partly Muir's exploration of what might have happened if the young Willa Anderson had married her 'Rugby champion and gone to live' in Montrose (1968, 125). Elizabeth carries an emotional force; she is a modernist heroine believing 'in something that flows through the universe . . . . It's not outside, it's *inside* oneself. And yet it comes suddenly, as if from outside' (73). She is shown working through the conflicts for an educated and intelligent young woman of that time, changing name, status and place by the act of marrying, who then sees the possibility of reclaiming her own identity only outwith Scotland: 'I could take my own name and leave Scotland' (124). Waking one morning beside Hector, she 'no longer knew who she was'; she moves into a hypnogogic state where the world stretched 'into dark impersonal nothingness and she herself was a terrifying anonymity' (64). The 'disordered puzzle of her identity' is that she is both Elizabeth Ramsay and Elizabeth Shand; she fears becoming more and more Elizabeth Shand and the years of the future assume the 'perspective of fields, each one separated by a fence from its neighbour . . . . This was no longer time or space, it was eternity; . . . perhaps a higher fence marked the boundary between life and death, but in the fields beyond it she was still Elizabeth Shand . . . . It was appalling' (65). Elizabeth's waking dream of this interminable succession of fences and fields, shows the landscapes of her married future as continuously contained and restricted. But she also knows that, like Hector, 'in the ultimate resort she too was simply herself' (65). Muir shows Elizabeth's feelings for Hector fluctuating wildly, making clear the strength of their sexual attraction and their lack of intellectual connection. It is Hector's presence that confuses Elizabeth's clarity; in his absence 'her painful agitation subsided with incredible quickness' (115) and she can sit down to read a book by the French philosopher, Henri Bergson. Elizabeth's intellectual excitement is calming for her and acts to remind us of her intelligence and connectedness to the intellectual currents of her time; but Muir also uses Bergson's ideas of motion and continuous change in the passage of time and the flux of consciousness (developed in works such as *Time and Free Will* [1910]) as an enabling image for Elizabeth's state of division: 'the whole of Elizabeth's world was in flux, although not exactly as Bergson had declared it to be, and instead of regarding the phenomenon with scientific interest she felt as if she were drowning in it' (115).

The Bergsonian idea of flux is opposed by the regulation of life by railway or school timetables, and of time itself by Greenwich mean time (introduced in 1884 in Britain). Sarah Murray's 'precisely regulated . . . scheme of life' had been imposed by her upbringing in her schoolteacher father's timetabled world; and Sarah is disturbed if she cannot predict 'what was to be seen at any hour of the day . . . the orderly life of Calderwick . . . keeping pace with the ordered march of the sun'. And it is Sarah who hears the 'prolonged whistle of the express from King's Cross . . . [p]unctual to the minute' (7), the train which is dropping the newly wed Hector and Elizabeth Shand into the mixture of Calderwick society. Her brother William has a more complicated relationship to time than Sarah, as befits the character whom Muir described as 'another version of Elizabeth in different circumstances' (Pick, ix). The 'large white dial of a clock' (68) facing the pulpit in William's church seems like Lawrence's 'great white clock–face . . . the eternal, mechanical, monotonous clock-face of time' in *Women in Love* (1921, 491; 1980, 523). But William stares at the clock's 'expressionless white circle' as he preaches not to regulate his time, but to lift himself through 'a kind of self-hypnosis . . . into a transcendental world favourable for sermons' (68). After his failure to help his brother Ned, and his spiritual crisis, William dreams of navigating himself on a tea-tray down a yellow river that is both in China and 'the river of the will of God' (272), interpreting it as the necessity of resigning himself to God's will. He continues a meditation on his dream as he struggles through the storm to see a parishioner, thinking of the 'stream of Time' and interpreting his dream sea as 'the Pacific, . . . almost smiling . . . . The sea of God's peace (273). William is thus shown as reaching a kind of resolution of his religious doubts through his dream, just before he falls into the 'nasty, stagnant corner' (44) of the docks where he drowns.

Elise too had dreamed of the sea, the Atlantic, where 'an enormous, endless billow' was going to obliterate the children and herself on the shore (242). Her fear on wakening is then superseded by a strengthened sense of herself as 'an unassailable point within the compass of her body, the centre . . . of a dimly perceived circle . . . . The centre of one's being, apparently, was both tranquil and intrusive' (242). Elise has a complicated function within the novel. She is both the younger Lizzie, reacting to the unfairness of her gendered upbringing, providing John Shand's emotional life in childhood and adulthood, and the sophisticated Elise who, through her early study of Saint-Simonianism and Enfantin (256), her relationship with Karl, and her talk of teleology which 'led to queer conclusions' (231), represents a questioning, radical, intellectual tradition, coming home to lay the ghost of her earlier self. She becomes a precipitating factor in the resolution of Hector and Elizabeth's relationship. Elizabeth is caught in a turmoil of feelings about being a married woman, about her essential identity, and is 'looking for her other self' when she first meets Elise: 'since Elise was a woman Elizabeth did not know that she fell in love with her at first sight' (165). This is the Elizabeth who has an out of body experience as an expression of poetic and intellectual passion, who feels split in the space of 'thickened obscurity' (174) between body and mind, who thinks of the 'impersonal force' of Hector's sexual appeal, his 'grace and strength' expressed in the language of the 'Song of Solomon' (175; *Bible* 7:4). Her revelations come through the medium and language of sexual orgasm, induced by masturbation: 'Elizabeth went on stroking her body, almost mechanically . . . an image of herself grew before her . . . . It was an overlapping of vibrations rather than a solid form, and the vibrations extended beyond the farthest stars. One end of this shadowy projection had long, slow, full waves; that was the body and its desires. At the other end were short quick waves; these represented the mind' (174). The frankness of Muir's approach to sexuality here prepares us for the possibility of Elizabeth and Elise's relationship. It is through Elise's money that Hector is enabled to leave Scotland for Singapore, Elise acknowledging to herself that she may just be 'buying off' Hector (257), leaving Elizabeth for her to sweep off to Europe, as a 'brand-new daughter, or sister, or wife, or whatever it was, having carried her off like a second Lochinvar' (278).

The ending of the novel refuses closure, the sexual possibilities widening beyond heterosexuality even as Elise acknowledges that Elizabeth may later return to some man 'the exact antithesis of Hector' (281). The train, representative early in the novel of the timetabled world, controlled by the clock, is the medium that carries Elise first out of mainland Europe into her past through geography and dreams, and then out of the past into alternate, uncertain and ambiguous futures which may carry new imprisonment: 'Calderwick receding farther and farther, for Ilye's conversation travelled even faster than the train . . . .[Muir's ellipses]' (281). The ending also becomes a movement into disconnection. Like the larks that had not even known it was Scotland at the beginning of the novel (2), Elise and Elizabeth fly off at the end into the world of not-Scotland. Freedom for them is flight from the constrictions of the known society into the privileged and detached life of incomers in southern France. But it is a flight to a continent about to be submerged in war and Muir implicitly uses knowledge of the outbreak of war to ensure uncertainty beyond the end of the novel.

For some readers, *Imagined Corners* is flawed by the intrusive narrator and the sense that it really does have enough 'material for two novels' in it, that Muir fails to join the two movements of her narrative, the external and internal, the sociological and the psychological[1]. A more positive reading is that Muir takes the disparate strands of her narrative and interweaves them so that the novel becomes the proper sum of its parts, the stresses and disjunctions between the outer and inner explorations symptomatic of the same stresses in society between the demands and repressions of the social structure and the inner worlds of the individual psyche. The main characters of the novel are shown as fragmented sites of conflict between competing selves, constructed in contradictory ways by the demands of societal expectations, their unconscious worlds clashing in dreams with their conscious realities. There is movement and fluidity, echoing Bergson's continuous change and flux, in the characters' understanding of their selves, a grasping after unity or sense while they fail to attain any stable understanding of their selves. Despite the critique of society apparent in the novel, Muir wanted to 'illumine life, not to reform it' (Pick, ix). The novel is a sophisticated enactment of the conflicts between societal repressions and individual yearning for escape, allowing her scope to explore the links between conscious and unconscious worlds, illuminating the dreaming of realities in *Imagined Corners*.

Note

1. Janet Caird, in particular, seems unconvinced that the novel is successful: 'a teasing, irritating book, because one is aware of possibilities in it not realised' (1992–93, 12).

Works Cited

Caird, Janet. 'Cakes Not Turned Willa Muir's Published Novels', *Chapman*. no.71. Winter 1992–93, 12–18

Eliot, T.S.'The Waste Land' in *Complete Poems and Plays*. London: Faber and Faber, 1969

Frazer, J. G. *The Golden Bough* [abridged edition]. London: MacMillan, 1922

Lawrence, D. H. *Women in Love*. London: Martin Secker, 1921; Harmondsworth: Penguin, 1980

Muir, Edwin *An Autobiography*. 1954; Edinburgh: Canongate, 1993

Muir, Willa *Belonging A Memoir*. London: Hogarth Press, 1968

Muir, Willa *Imagined Corners* in *Imagined Selves*. 1931; Edinburgh: Canongate, 1995

Pick, J. B. 'Introduction' to *Imagined Corners*. Edinburgh: Canongate, 1987

Woolf, Virginia 'Modern Fiction' in *The Common Reader*. London: Hogarth Press, 1925; also in *Essays of Virginia Woolf*. Andrew McNeillie ed. London: Hogarth Press, 1994, vol. 4

'An ordinary little girl'?
Willa Muir's *Mrs Ritchie*

Beth Dickson

If *Imagined Corners* (1931) is considered, in part, as a study of what happened to Scottish women who rejected the gender roles which their early twentieth-century provincial society offered them, then *Mrs Ritchie* can be seen as what happened to one woman who accepted them. Though the title seems superficially to consist merely of a name, it is also the role which masks the identity of Muir's anti-heroine, Annie Rattray, a little girl from the wrong side of the tracks who grows up looking for security in respectability, willing to use her supreme powers of determination to recreate herself in society's image of womanhood. Tragically what is produced is not an ideal woman, but a monster. *Mrs Ritchie* shows how gender is socially constructed in its treatment of Annie herself, of Miss Julia, and eventually of Annie's daughter, Sarah Annie.

The reader is introduced to eleven-year-old Annie Rattray on her way home from school. Her father, a drunken ne'er-do-weel, has appeared at the school playground embarrassing Annie, who is overtaken by rage of an intensity which would be disturbing even in an adult. She fantasises that she can control the weather in a cold landscape, 'her rage drove the hail until it was lashing her father and her sister on their naked, shivering bodies. This eased her suffocation' (5). After this vision of Annie's rage, Muir moves with grim irony to a description of her external appearance: 'just an ordinary little girl, one would have said, in a dark blue pinafore and black-ribbed stockings pulled up over her bony knees, with a checked canvas school-bag swinging from her left shoulder' (6). Anything less 'ordinary' than Annie Rattray's tendencies to rage, her desires for supremacy and corresponding desires to subjugate her relatives would be hard to imagine. The town of Calderwick ostensibly espouses the cult of domesticity which views women as angels in the home, guardians of morality and family life and repositories of gentleness, kindness, self-effacement, indeed, self-sacrifice.The gulf between Annie's naked assertion of ego and the role which society constructs for her seems unbridgeable.

In addition to her violent fantasies of dominance, Annie compensates for her poor background by doing well at school where her desires to 'beat' people transmute into the socially acceptable forms of coming first in class tests. However, her prize for this achievement is a cookery book, awarded by Mr Laing who 'thought how ignorant she was of her destiny as a woman' (14). Muir's ever-present irony awards him 'perhaps . . . a moment of compunction' (14) before making this choice of prize-book. It is through such individual moments of social compliance that gender roles are fixed. Another teacher, Mr Boyd, offers Annie the chance to win a bursary and continue her education at the Academy. It is Annie's mother who refuses this offer in terms of conventional gender expectations: 'It's no' even as if you were a laddie. Na, na, my leddy, the minute you're fourteen you gang to a job, or else you'll gie me a hand here wi' the washin' and the hoose' (23). Being thwarted thus provokes Annie to paroxysms of rage and she returns in her dreams to the cold landscape: 'she was walking on thick cold clear ice, beneath which the faces of her mother, her father and Mary looked up at her. She stamped upon them' (25).

Annie embarks on a period of anarchy, losing her place in class and becoming a ring-leader in playground games. However, her position is precarious and when one of her friends accuses her of acting like her father, games lose their attraction for Annie and she withdraws, feeling despairing and suicidal. Resisting this urge, Annie renounces the individualism which has brought her so close to destruction in order to gain secure, respectable status. She adopts God as her father and sees in the church a replacement for school as the institution which awards the prize of social respectability. This is a moment of personal defeat which is utterly destructive for Annie and those with whom she is intimately linked.

By the end of Book I of the novel, Muir has shown the extent to which Annie's gender identity has been constructed for her principally through the difficulties women had at this time in gaining access to the higher education which would lead to more interesting and financially rewarding forms of work than the laundry-service Annie performs at home. In Book II, Muir looks more closely at Annie's sexual identity. In Book I, Annie had observed her father in a boisterous sexually-motivated game with a younger woman. From this, Annie transfers her dislike of her father and her related dislike of the dirt and mess of poverty onto sex. This dislike is encapsulated in her hatred of human hair which sometimes denotes sexuality and sometimes power. Such issues become intextricably linked with religion.

Annie goes to work as a maid in the house of, significantly, her Sunday School teacher, Miss Julia Carnegie. She is drawn to Miss Julia, 'a lady dedicated to the domestic altar and the sacred hearth of home' (57). Through this character Muir examines the role of what she characterises in *Women: An Inquiry* as the 'superfluous woman' (1925; 1996, 5). Though Julia fills her time helping foreign missionary organisations this does not seem to channel her energy as effectively as going to auctions does for her sister Susan. Julia's objects in the drawing room are a suggestive collection of High Victorian clutter: 'the piano, the books of poetry in limp leather bindings, the ivory pagoda beside the ebony elephants, and, of course, all the palms and arum lilies, were Miss Julia's' (70).

Annie likes the drawing-room best. It is a 'Sabbath room' where there is an ordered tranquillity. It seems to sum up the link between religious observance and respectability. But for two reasons it is a pseudo-Eden. Firstly, like Annie's fantasies of domination which literally 'froze' her enemies, the drawing room is only perfect because it too is frozen and unlived in. Annie's ideal of perfection is a vision of paralysis which has no room for anything as messy as humanity; she becomes most annoyed when her mistresses move any of the drawing room objects. Secondly, the drawing-room's seeming tranquillity is imposed by Annie's desire to control everything and becomes disordered in the scenes in which Annie helps Miss Julia with her missionary work. There the atmosphere is heavy with a repressed sexuality:

> The map of Africa became a dark blot on the round belly of the earth, a devil's mark upon the belly of the earth. Annie and Miss Julia drew closer to each other over the polished table, and in their virgin minds hippopotami rolled their vast bulk, crocodiles heaved their obscene heads, insatiable lions sprang from cover, and cruelty, lewdness and murder roamed unchecked. It was a hot, savage night of lust that Miss Julia called up (71-2).

The recent upsurge of study in issues connected with empire has alerted critics to the fact that textual references to countries in the Two Thirds world are neither as neutral nor as insignificant as they have previously been interpreted to be. Edward Said has said that the critical task is to 'describe [the experience of empire] as pertaining to Indians *and* Britishers, Algerians *and* French, Westerners *and* Africans' (1993, xxiv). Empire forms a constant, if fitfully expressed, background in *Mrs Ritchie*, in particular the 'scramble for Africa' which took place in the last third of the nineteenth century. From *Mrs Ritchie* it seems clear that Muir's repudiation of the values of Victorian and Edwardian Britain, which characterised most modernist writers, extends to her attitude to Empire. The whole presupposition of Empire is called ironically in doubt when Miss Julia is asked by Annie for a volume of missionary stories in the naive but nonetheless preposterous question, '[p]lease, Miss Julia, can I have Africa?' (71).

Muir's exploration of religion leads her to a consideration of the link between Empire and missionary work. The attitudes to Africa held by Miss Julia are given through indirect narration of her thoughts. Julia's understanding of Africa has been formed by the stories of missionary work published by the London Missionary Society. One story in particular of a slave mother escaping from a lion in the jungle and reaching a mission station in safety is Annie's favourite and is mentioned twice (16, 71). This story performs two functions: it externalises Annie's desire to dominate as she admires the slave mother for getting the better of the lion, and it is used to indicate Miss Julia's suppressed sexuality. Here Muir, who read and taught psychology, may be following Freud's use of Africa in its Western appellation the 'Dark Continent' as a metaphor for female sexuality in *The Question of Lay Analysis* (1925–1926). Two narratives are being blocked here. What was the slave-mother's story? And was the involvement of nineteenth century Scotswomen in missionary work merely a narrative of repression? There is not room here to give such questions the depth and breadth of intellectual consideration that they deserve. Nevertheless, the point can be briefly made that the use of an African slave woman's short narrative as a metaphor for the rage and frustrated sexuality of free white women is entirely problematic, showing the customary hierarchy of white over black, where black is used only to define white.

Miss Julia's relationship with Annie has to compensate for her lack of fulfilment in life. Not only is Julia seeking a vicarious experience of motherhood, she is also looking for a sexual confidante. She feels guilty about being 'so intimate with a servant' (78), reminding us that Annie's class is another complicating element in Muir's exploration of her identity. But when Julia begins to make more emotional demands on Annie, Annie, because of Julia's continual discussion of sex, begins to consider her own sexual future. Resenting Julia's request for sympathy, Annie responds in a masculinised way: 'her shoulder grew hard and resistant under Miss Julia's pressure; she would have liked to shake off the hand that rested there' (92). Annie perceives virginity, especially when overlaid with same-sex affection, as some sort of failure. Though admirable because it is untouched like the drawing room through the week, virginity is incompatible with the final social respectability of having a man at the head of the pew.

It is with this in mind that Annie marries Johnny Ritchie, the joiner who is 'emotionally maimed', as David Robb points out (1990, 151). Again for Annie religion and respectability are closely linked. She believes that the sexual act, though necessary for procreation, is a devil's wile, because of its resistance to control and the inevitable abandonment involved. Much of the book's significance lies in its powerful metaphors, as when the house is used metaphorically to suggest repression and resistance when the marriage is consummated: 'but the warmth . . . remained locked away and inaccessible, locked up like the prim, clean house, and to the door that guarded it Johnny Ritchie could not find the key' (126). The text hanging above the marital bed which shows the rays of God's eye makes Annie think 'her inner eye must be as the eye of God; like his it must penetrate to the remotest corners of her body, unsleeping, vigilant, irradiating the whole of it so that it became a fit garment for a daughter of God' (123). Annie is 'given' in marriage by no one, least of all herself. The only 'penetration' she experiences is her own unsleeping scrutiny of her actions and motives. She wants the social status a marriage contract will give her but resolutely abjures its claims of profound mutuality. The gulf between the wild aggressive person she is and the gentle, submissive gender role she adopts is vast. Only a prodigious amount of self-control and determination could prevent the human personality from cracking up under the strain of it.

Johnny Ritchie suffers under Annie's domineering rule. The children when they arrive are likewise forbidden to deviate from Annie's regime. In his youth John Samuel begins to rebel by coming in late after visiting a local family, the Reids, whose life is warm and easy-going, all that Annie's is not. Provoked beyond endurance he declares that he wishes he had been born a Reid: 'Mrs Ritchie's self-control almost deserted her. She stepped forward as if to fell John Samuel to the ground, and he, fending her off like a cornered animal, flung her from him with all his force' (184–5). Violence seethes behind the facade of the docile mother and the narrator concludes with the key point that: 'she was not his mother; she was not Mrs Ritchie; she was a secretive, rigid, assertive individual called Annie' (190).

This violence is expressed openly after Johnny Ritchie and John Samuel have died, when there is nothing to stop Annie battering her daughter as part of her campaign to possess the house, a design in which she has been thwarted by her husband's ineffectiveness and her son's deliberate awkwardness. Although Sarah Annie, influenced by the suffragette movement, sees how much her mother has been thwarted by a repressive system, she

cannot withstand her mother's desire to dominate. Finally she leaves 'home'
and Mrs Ritchie is left in possession, solicitously tending the graves of her
husband and son who in death offer no check to her ambition. The violence
of the 'ordinary little girl' is thus incorporated into that monstrous creation,
'Mrs Ritchie'.

The scene in the kitchen where Mrs Ritchie tries to attack John Samuel
seems closely linked by incident and theme to George Douglas Brown's *The
House with the Green Shutters*. Both novels share main characters who wield
power which comes neither from their minds nor their emotions, but their
wills. For both characters their individuality is expressed in their houses.
Gourlay is always improving his and Mrs Ritchie keeps hers spotlessly clean.
Both Gourlay and Mrs Ritchie use their houses to chart their social position
in a society which has somehow rejected them: Gourlay is aware that others
see him as a slow thinker and talker and Mrs Ritchie has been forced into
accepting a domestic role because society has refused her any other. Both
Gourlay and Mrs Ritchie feel that their houses prove others' estimation
of them wrong. Both have struggled to achieve, and now hold, what they
think of as a natural position of domination over their neighbours. While
both Brown and Muir show Gourlay and Mrs Ritchie to be individuals
possessing an irreducible minimum of personality, and who are responsible
for their own actions, both authors are also interested in the way in which
these personalities are substantially acted upon or constructed by society.

Society's effect on these characters through its institutions such as church
and education, commonly held to constitute a distinct national identity,
underlies both novels. As far as Gourlay senior is concerned the institutions
are of no relevance to him. They neither regulate his rise to prominence, nor
referee his fall. That is checked only by market forces. When his gathered
capital and willpower are enough to drive competition aside, he prospers.
When industrialisation begins to make itself felt in Ayrshire, he does not
have the business acumen to prosper, so he becomes prey to his enemies.
The institutions are important to him only in so far as they offer his son the
possibility of a professional career which would restore the family fortunes.
If Gourlay is not openly critical of institutions, Brown is implicitly showing
laissez-faire institutions which fail to curb the destructive social patterns associated with business life. Gourlay's success has been identified with power
and dominance, conventionally conceived as aspects of masculinity. When
he fails, Gourlay is publicly humiliated by his neighbours and though he
controls himself at the time, the real damage which has been done to him
is seen in the violence with which he treats his disgraced son who returns
to Barbie after being expelled from University:

To break a man's spirit so, take that from him which he will never
recover while he lives, send him slinking away animo castrato – for
that is what it comes to – is a sinister outrage of the world. It is as
bad as the rape of a woman, and ranks with the sin against the Holy
Ghost, derives from it, indeed. Yet this was the outrage Gourlay meant
to work upon his son (1901, 210–11).

Brown's language here interlinks religion and gender in ways that show
the corruption of Gourlay's moral sense, emblematic of the whole society's
corruption.

Muir's novel, like Brown's, attacks the establishment; Muir's critique of
institutions, both education and the church, is that they repress women.
Specifically, Muir's most serious charge against the church is that it is satisfied by, or taken in by, outward, rather than inward, conformity to its
teaching. In Annie Rattray this leads to exactly the same horror as it does
in Robert Wringhim, the anti-hero of James Hogg's *The Private Memoirs
and Confessions of a Justified Sinner*. Annie looks to religion for the social
respectability on which her personal security depends. However, her appro-
priation of the tenets of the faith is so corrupted by her own need that what
she exhibits is in every way a denial of what she is supposed to be practising.
Her duties to her husband are ways of manipulating him to become more
respectable, and her care for her children is a reign of terror in which she
seeks to extirpate every human desire or inclination they may have.

Mrs Ritchie's monstrous personality dwarfs the other characters in the
novel, prompting intertextual comparisons with novels commonly held to
form an important Scottish tradition, novels such as Scott's *Redgauntlet*,
Hogg's *Confessions*, Stevenson's *The Master of Ballantrae*, as well as
Brown's *The House with the Green Shutters* already noted. In this tradition, *Mrs Ritchie* can be read as a counter-narrative which opposes these
classic literary versions of Scottish masculinity, particularly as seen in *The
House with the Green Shutters*: what we see in John Gourlay *cannot* be
essentially masculine because his every tendency to destructive behaviour
is mirrored in variety and matched in degree by Mrs Ritchie's. These two
novels can be used to raise questions about gender and national identity.
Are John Gourlay and Mrs Ritchie somehow being 'more' Scottish than
the characters of Muir's *Imagined Corners*, for instance? Might there be a
link between nationality and violence, given that both Gourlay and Ritchie
resort frequently to violence of differing kinds? In these novels Brown and
Muir both seem to present violence as an intrinsic part of the repressive
and damaging nature of Scottish society.

Both novelists are critical of Scottish institutions but for somewhat different reasons. Brown implies that institutions are weak or corrupt in the face of the dehumanising effects of industrialisation. Muir sees institutions as having too much power and in *Mrs Grundy in Scotland* welcomes the coming of secularism, where increasing prosperity loosens dependence on tradition (1936; 1996, 84–5). Yet if the analyses of social pressures and flaws are different in these two novels, the tendency to violence of the two central characters connects them with each other and then more widely with Scottish fiction's gallery of demons. Larger than life, wilful, violent and evil, Mrs Ritchie and John Gourlay are comparable with Redgauntlet, Robert Wringhim, James Ballantrae and Dr Jekyll and Mr Hyde. Religion is one of the threads connecting these figures. But as far as Brown is concerned Christianity is a dead letter in Barbie. Although he uses imagery of supernatural evil to describe the enraged Gourlay, its complement is neither the theological evil explored by Hogg, nor the quizzical moral evil of Stevenson, but an entirely secular phenomenon of a society-without-'god'. Brown uses the imagery of the older emanations of evil but avoids their religious presuppositions. Muir indicts repressive religion and a society so determined on the pursuit of righteousness that every individual must devote his or her entire life to securing that goal. She shows religion as fertile soil for psychological disturbance.

Violence is the gateway between the 'this-worldly' self and the demonic 'other-wordly' self. That Mrs Ritchie has such a demonic other self is demonstrated in John Samuel's wartime obsession that: 'every soldier in the barrage, French or German or British, was suffering like him from his mother's anger – as if *she* were the earth that spewed out death at them, as if she had blasted the trees and darkened the sky and twisted the acres of wire' (254–5). Muir uses Mrs Ritchie, 'really only a bony little woman in a black dress' (255), to represent for John Samuel evil so passionate and powerful it could consume a continent. Though Muir had asserted in *Women: an Inquiry* that women as a sex were specially responsible for creativity (1925; 1996, 8–16), she had also written there that women's concern was primarily

human affairs and experiences, material which helps them more capably to scrutinise, to interpret, and to meddle with the people they meet. The result is that they often meddle tediously with other people's lives. Like Hedda Gabler, they must have their fingers in somebody's destiny, destructively if not creatively. Destruction of this kind instead of creation is tragic, but it arises at least from a pre-occupation with humanity, and so, unlike war, it is womanly (1925; 1996, 14).

This seems to prefigure the tragic construction of Mrs Ritchie as the Mother-Destroyer. The character of Mrs Ritchie is a ferocious attack on the Scottish society which had produced her, just as insidious in her natural and supernatural dimensions as any of her male counterparts. The analysis of gender construction places the novel squarely in a 'this-worldly' tradition yet the transformation of Mrs Ritchie into a 'priestess' (251) of evil relates to older, 'other-worldly' and darker traditions in Scottish life.

Mrs Ritchie is sometimes thought to be less imaginatively successful than *Imagined Corners*. The earlier novel studies repression and its effects through a wide spectrum of differing characters; the focus moves from telescopic to panoramic, from conscious to unconscious. In *Mrs Ritchie*, Muir turns this around and, by concentrating on Mrs Ritchie herself, puts under the microscope the damage done by repression to the human spirit, and that done by repressed anger to the surrounding people, hardly relieved by any hope or possibility of release. In *Mrs Ritchie* she is working through the issue of gender construction, as she does in *Imagined Corners*. *Mrs Ritchie* also raises questions for the critic of its relation to a Scottish tradition in fiction. Muir's portrayal of the forces which make Annie Rattray into Mrs Ritchie challenges readers to reflect critically on social expectations of women. Muir's novel also encourages readers to ask searching critical questions about the nature of the Scottish literary tradition. The novel is finally bitterly critical about the way Scotland represses women. The flight of the intelligent woman from Scotland which is the ending of *Imagined Corners* is echoed more tragically in the flight of Sarah Annie at the end of *Mrs Ritchie* from her mother and all the forces of repression Annie Ritchie represents. Muir's second (and last published) novel is a sombre, shrewd and challenging work of fiction.

Works Cited

Brown, George Douglas *The House with the Green Shutters*. J. T. Low ed. with introduction and notes. 1901; Edinburgh: Holmes McDougall, 1974

Muir, Willa *Imagined Corners* in *Imagined Selves*. 1931; Edinburgh: Canongate, 1996

Muir, Willa *Mrs Grundy in Scotland* in *Imagined Selves*. 1936; Edinburgh: Canongate, 1996

Muir, Willa *Mrs Ritchie* in *Imagined Selves*. 1933; Edinburgh: Canongate, 1996

Muir, Willa *Women: An Inquiry* in *Imagined Selves*. 1925; Edinburgh: Canongate, 1996

Robb, David S. 'The Published Novels of Willa Muir' in *Studies in Scottish Fiction: Twentieth Century*. Horst W. Drescher and Joachim Schwend eds. Frankfurt Am Main: 1990, 149–161

Said, Edward W. *Culture and Imperialism*. London: Chatto & Windus, 1993

Nancy Brysson Morrison (1903–86)

Nancy Brysson Morrison was born in Glasgow in 1903; all of her three sisters and two of her three brothers became writers in adult life. She was educated at Park School for Girls in Glasgow and Harvington College in London. She did not marry and her life was spent mainly in Glasgow and latterly in Edinburgh and London, where she moved to be near one of her brothers. When she died in 1986, her ashes were brought north to her sister Mary's grave in Deeside. Apart from *The Gowk Storm*, Nancy Brysson Morrison's novels are now all out of print. She was, however, recognised as a writer of significance in her own time. *The Gowk Storm* was a Book Society Choice when it was first published in 1933 and *The Winnowing Years*, 1949, won the first Frederick Niven Award. In the 1930s, Edwin Muir classed her fiction with that of Gunn, Gibbon and Willa Muir, and in the 1950s Dr James Michie of Aberdeen University, who later became her literary executor, taught her work in his Scottish Literature courses. Although the lives of women are foregrounded in many of her novels, she deals also with themes of Scottish history and religion, with philosophical determinism and with the use of the Scots language, all of which concerns relate her work to the Scottish fiction tradition. Her first novel *Breakers*, 1930, contains a Highland Clearances episode which predates Gunn's *Butcher's Broom* by four years and must be among the earliest portrayals of the Clearances in Scottish fiction. Her biographical study *Mary Queen of Scots*, in which she stresses the predetermined nature of Mary's journey to her ending at Fotheringay, won a Literary Guild Award when it was published in 1960. She also wrote radio plays, including *True Minds* about Jane Welsh Carlyle (16 Oct. 1954, Scottish Home Service). She wrote twenty eight romantic novels, 1942–59, under the name of Christine Stathern. Nancy Brysson Morrison's literary papers are now deposited in the National Library of Scotland in Edinburgh.

M.P.M.

Poetic Narrative in Nancy Brysson Morrison's *The Gowk Storm*

Margery Palmer McCulloch

In her 1929 essay 'Women and Fiction', Virginia Woolf expressed the view that 'it is in poetry that women's fiction is still weakest' and that it is only when this 'poetic spirit' has been encouraged that women writers will be able to look beyond their personal preoccupations 'to the wider questions which the poet tries to solve – of our destiny and the meaning of life' (Woolf, 1929; 1979, 51). Nancy Brysson Morrison's *The Gowk Storm*, published in 1933, four years after Woolf's essay, fulfils Woolf's demand for poetry in fiction. It is this poetic discourse and its critical perspective on the historical and patriarchal society depicted in the narrative which will be the principal focus of this essay.

The Gowk Storm is the story of three sisters living with their parents in an isolated manse on the edge of the Highlands. In particular, it is the story of the attempt by two of these sisters to live their lives according to their own wishes and values, values which are seen to run counter to those of the dominant social order of the time. Although no precise period for the setting is given, several references in the text suggest a date around the 1850s or 1860s. In the Prologue, for example, Nannie is described as having been nurse to the girls' mother and her eight brothers and sisters 'when the nineteenth century had been as youthful as they' (1), while in the Epilogue the father has answered a call to a church beside Glasgow Green 'which had been a Relief church before the Union in 1847' (177), a date which the narrator mentions as if it is within her memory. Other textual details similarly suggest a setting not much later than the mid-point of the century.

The Gowk Storm is outstanding for its author's handling of narrative form. The story is told retrospectively through the memories of the youngest sister Lisbet and is framed by a Prologue and Epilogue, also spoken by Lisbet. Throughout the text, this retrospective narrative pattern is punctuated by images or happenings which foreshadow the tragedies to come. The first person narrative form with its necessarily limited perspective provides a source of tension in that Lisbet often reports what as a young girl she has seen but has not fully understood, thus leaving the reader to complete a scenario without the help of an omniscient narrator or shifts in focalisation; at other times Lisbet communicates an interpretation which comes from her mature self as she sees more deeply into past events and their significance. Of especial importance in this formal organisation is the poetic nature of the narrative and the perspectives it offers.

This imagistic approach is present from the outset. The Prologue begins with an evocation of the manse garden of Lisbet's childhood: '[e]verything grew a little wildly in that muffled, breathless place. All the trees' strength went into their straggling height and each one seemed to be stretching upwards in an attempt to see over its neighbour's untidy head' (1). At this early stage, the reader is unable to relate the Hardyesque description to the lives of the daughters of the manse, although the atmosphere of unease is acknowledged. As the plot develops, however, the metaphor of the muffled garden becomes only too clear. Chapter One deepens the elegiac mood of the Prologue with its opening descriptive references to a sky 'lit by chance rays from some other world'; the snow streaking the mountains 'like the skeletons of huge, prehistoric animals'. To Lisbet it seems 'as though, in those transient windless seconds between dawn and daylight, the world had resolved itself again into the countours and substances that composed it before man trod on its earth and drank in its air' (7). This suggestion of human life itself being transient continues as Lisbet tells of reading the ballad 'The Unquiet Grave' from her *Book of Songs* as she waits for breakfast, a tale of lost love, tragic death and a spirit which cannot find rest (Grigson, 1975, 93). In Lisbet's narration, therefore, we early become aware of an elegiac and fated note, the sense of a story being communicated by someone who holds the tragic ending in her mind and heart.

In contrast to the sombre key of Lisbet's opening narration is Chapter One's vibrant characterisation of family members as they gather for breakfast. Emmy's late arrival and her quickness of retort identify her as animated, imaginative and potentially rebellious. Julia is lively-minded too, but in this opening chapter her qualities are discovered in the clever way she diverts her father's attention from Emmy's wilfulness, reading his character shrewdly and leading him back to the safe topic of his well-chosen sermon text. The father himself is economically yet forcefully presented through his curt words to Emmy and his obvious self-interest as a cold, detached man with little consideration of the wishes or needs of others. This impression is sustained through Lisbet's narrative comments and through her fear that Emmy's muttered protests might burst out into a more open confrontation. For what we understand from this short scene is that, although outnumbered by the women around him and uninvolved in the day-to-day running of the household, the father is the ultimate power in the family's life, wielding that power without consultation where he considers it necessary. Throughout the plot the mother is curiously absent in the lives of her daughters. In this first scene she is viewed through Lisbet's consciousness and, like Juley, the mother in Catherine Carswell's *Open the Door!*, she would appear to have taken refuge in religion. Lisbet comments:

> She was still a handsome woman although she no longer paid any attention to her appearance. Looking back now, I realise, when I think of her carefree upbringing and lively youth, how uneventfully the days must have passed in the Barnfingal manse yet she accepted them without question or regret, and never thought of herself as other than happy. But as she sewed at the parlour fire or sat at the table covering Nannie's jam pots (she sat to do most things nowadays), memories must have flickered in and out of her mind, like moths uneasily attracted to a candle flame, until she would feel life was leaving her with nothing but anniversaries (7–8).

Lisbet's retrospective evaluation adds to the atmosphere of restriction around the women, despite the liveliness of their talk, a restraint foreshadowed in the earlier imagistic description of the setting. The uncertain mood continues after the father's departure in the girls' discussion of his Sunday text: '[b]e thou faithful unto death, and I will give thee a crown of life' (9). It is the religious mother who insists on the text having a meaning beyond this world as 'immortality', while Emmy emphasises its worldliness in the injunction to be faithful *unto death*. In this opening scene, Emmy's directness, her liveliness and creativity and what we feel is her justified rebelliousness, draw the reader towards her, even as concern for her is stirred by Lisbet's strange comment that the piano is so associated with Emmy that 'if any one else had touched its yellowed keys, no matter where her spirit lay, it would quiveringly awake and her fingers tremble to feel them once again' (10).

From the Prologue and Chapter One, then, one can already appreciate the significance of the poetic or imagistic dimension in the narrative in the way it creates mood and releases implications in characterisation and happening. In this respect, weather imagery and imagery of the natural world generally are especially meaningful. The isolation of the tree-shrouded manse, dank and low-lying, is pierced by walks to the schoolhouse in the clachan of Barnfingal and by occasional outings to the home of the neighbouring Strathern family. Lisbet describes their progress from the manse through the shaded wood on their first visit to the Stratherns and how as they walk uphill to the gate 'the sun struck wildly between the trees' (21). This sudden image of freedom is continued in her perception of the unfamiliarity of the familiar as they pass through the customary landscape in the carriage, as opposed to on foot: 'I felt the road that afternoon was like a shrunken measuring-tape. The kindly sun glanced on the sullen hill-tops and lit up every blade of grass growing from the tussocky dykes' (21). Although the connection with the Strathern family ultimately turns out tragically, at this point the imagery of the journey to the Strathern home contrasts with the muffled darkness of the manse's setting, telling its own story of the girls' lives, their capacity for openness and vitality and the contrary constricted nature of their everyday existence. Similarly, contrasting responses to stormy weather chart the changes in their lives. In Chapter Two of Book One, when her older sisters have gone to the Stratherns' ball, Lisbet lies in bed 'listening to the scraping winds and piping creatures of the night'. She hears the wind blow a branch of the fir tree against the window 'making a sound like small tapping fingers' (14). She is secure within the noises of the old house with the storm outside and hopes Julia will not have the branch cut down as she has threatened to do. Later, however, when Julia's loving relationship with the schoolmaster has been brought to an end, the storm-bound house holds no comfort for Lisbet in the face of Julia's grief:

On Hallowe'en the three of us sat with Nannie in the kitchen. Outside, spirits, released for one night in the year, rode on the wind, rending the trees in their fury. The window darkened as their shadow spasms crossed it and we could hear them cracking and groaning . . . . I no longer exulted with the storm in the glory of its strength; it sounded piteous to me now, the shutout, unhappy wind. Unlikely things happened in this world – might take place perhaps before the kettle came to the boil, and the storm gusts rattling at the door were like some one trying to get in (91–2).

Here, with its resonances of *Wuthering Heights*, the storm acts as an objective correlative for the passions in the human scene and emphasises that all is not as it should be in the lives of the sisters.

The story of Julia's love for the Catholic dominie, Mr MacDonald, is the principal matter of Books One and Two of the novel and for Edwin Morgan, in his 'Introduction' to the 1988 Canongate reprint, this love affair illustrates the relevance of its metaphorical stormy-weather title. For Morgan, 'Julia's crisis turned out to be a gowk-storm crisis, swift and bleak but not long-lasting; soon after it she marries . . . a widower with two grown-up sons and a grown-up daughter, and . . . settles down to an acceptable existence' (ix). Like Julia's mother, he would appear to view this outcome as 'a very suitable marriage' (95). This is a reading which conforms to the conventions of the nineteenth-century novel in regard to the depiction of the lives of young women, where an unsuitable alliance is recognised in time for the mistaken match it is, thus allowing a more appropriate marriage to take place – a triumph of sense over sensibility. Despite Edwin Morgan's own qualities as poet, it is also a reading which ignores the impact of the poetic discourse of this twentieth-century novel whose imagery releases new perspectives on the events being narrated, perspectives which derive from the author's awareness of the changes which have taken place in women's lives since the mid-nineteenth century but which run counter to the conventions of the patriarchal society in which the novel is set. If the imagery of the text is given proper attention, the depiction of Julia's love affair with the schoolmaster reads quite differently. Thus, before her father has had the dominie evicted from his charge and from the community, Lisbet, who accompanies the lovers on their meetings, remembers 'Julia's voice thrilling with laughter, and saw them come towards me. She had taken off her bonnet and the unbridled wind swept through her hair, drawn back from her brow, as she jumped from tussock to tussock, her hand in his' (60). The detail of the descriptive imagery and the rhythms of the prose, at first flowing freely, then broken up by the punctuation to pattern her jumping motion, convey freedom, energy, joy. Later, when her father has made his malign power felt, personally and publicly, it is again the imagery and the slow, stilted rhythmic movement which communicate her emotional desolation: 'Julia's mind had gone like ice. We who lived with her could make no impression upon it. Our comfort, our moods, our thoughts, did not touch her; she was locked within her numbed self beyond our reach'. Lisbet is 'appalled' by 'the dreariness of her voice when she made the remark about winter . . . . I had been so ready to believe that at last the past was being forgotten and now, for one bared second, I glimpsed the gaping emptiness of her out-

look' (94). The wrong which has been done to Julia and the *unsuitability*
of the eventual marriage to the widower Edwin is again communicated imagistically. Lisbet notices that in the 'general merriment' surrounding the
marriage 'Julia seemed oddly out of tune' (96). She bursts into tears the
night before her wedding as she prepares for bed with her sisters. Lisbet
remembers: 'I felt I would have done anything in this world to escape from
that broken weeping, those gasping breaths between her sobs. I have never
seen her cry since' (105). Julia is changed after her marriage, easily irritated
yet conforming more passively to society's expectations than we would have
expected from our earlier knowledge of her; unable or unwilling to notice
the crisis brewing between her step-daughter, Christine, and Stephen and
Emmy, or to consider it other than conventionally when it boils over. Yet,
in opposition to Edwin Morgan's interpretation, I would argue that this
change is not communicated to us as 'maturity', as a successful entry into
the adult dominant order of society. If, to follow the Marxist critic Pierre
Macherey, we read in this novel 'the text [which] says what it does not say'
(1966, 82–93), then we can be in no doubt that Julia's entry into the adult
world as a wife has been achieved at the expense of her own female identity
and female values and that, in her, as in the patriarchal society which orders
how things should be, the female principle has once more been suppressed.
As the plot develops in relation to the life of the second sister, Emmy, we
realise how deeply ironic in relation to the events of the plot as a whole
the title of this novel is, encapsulating as it does, not what the dictionary
and epigraph denote as 'a storm of several days at the end of April or the
beginning of May; an evil or abstract obstruction of short duration', but
a series of crises and an encompassing system of values which bring about
the destruction of the essential self of one sister and the deaths of another
sister and a friend. Nothing could be of longer duration.

In her essay on the life and work of Sylvia Plath, 'A Fine, White Flying
Myth', Sandra M. Gilbert discusses images of entrapment and freedom in
writing by women and how through these images 'the story told is invariably
a story of being trapped, by society or by the self as an agent of society,
and then somehow escaping or trying to escape' (Gilbert and Gubar, 1979,
251). In Catherine Carswell's *Open the Door!*, the freeing by Joanna and
Aunt Perdy of the birds caught by the fowlers is one such imagistic episode,
symbolising both Joanna's 'escape' from her first marriage as a consequence
of her husband's accidental death and the fact that she has escaped with
wings undamaged; she is free to try again to find a flight path to individual
identity and fulfilment (Carswell, 1920; 1996, 142). In *The Gowk Storm*,
on the other hand, the imagery is of entrapment. It occurs in two separate

incidents in the novel. In the first, Emmy returns from a month-long visit to Julia's new home bearing a bird in a cage. She tells Lisbet that she had found this beside a wishing pool close to the Strathern house and it is clear that she believes it to have been left for her deliberately by Stephen Wingate, the fiancé of Edwin's daughter, Christine. The narrative has already signalled obliquely Stephen's attraction to Emmy, and Emmy herself has confessed to Lisbet her warmth towards him. Introduced at this point, the caged bird becomes more than an intriguing incident along the storyline and takes on a negative symbolic force, pointing to an unhappy situation which cannot be resolved without hurt to one or more of the three young people involved. Emmy's acceptance of the gift prefigures the situation that she and Stephen ultimately find themselves in: 'like an unsuspecting person caught unawares in a trap of circumstance', as Lisbet later is to say of Stephen (140). The bird symbol therefore also has resonances of vulnerability, of the caging being imposed upon the youthful protagonists by external forces that they cannot see or guard against. For what context and image foreground is the debilitating power of social convention and a social hypocrisy which would rather shut all three young people into distorted love relationships than openly break an engagement which has proved to be mistaken. Christine has so internalised the social status of marriage and the horror with which society would regard a broken engagement and jilted woman, that she would rather marry Stephen knowing that he no longer loved her than allow the marriage to be called off. Lisbet had at their first meeting characterised Christine Strathern as having features 'so indeterminate that they made no impression upon me; they were like a wax-doll's which have melted ever so slightly at the fire' (19) – a metaphorical description which captures her lack of individuality, her inability to be her own person as Emmy so clearly is with her quick tongue, rational mind and musical creativity. Ultimately Christine chooses death by drowning as opposed to the perceived disgrace of being rejected, while Emmy and Stephen impetuously attempt elopement since there appears to be no possible prospect of their marriage being considered acceptable.

The second appearance of the caged bird imagery occurs when Lisbet is visiting Julia and Edwin and overhears them speak together of Christine and her clinging behaviour towards her fiancé: 'it's a symptom of insecurity', Julia comments. 'She should be told that if you keep the cage door open, the bird is not nearly so likely to fly away' (127). Julia speaks here of Christine and her obsessive caging of Stephen, but the metaphor could equally be applied to her own situation with Edwin. 'She was buttonholing and her thread had become twisted: I watched her let her needle hang to twirl it unwound' (127). Lisbet's comment reminds us of the manner in which Julia's youthful love has been destroyed and suggests how often she may have felt herself trapped in her 'acceptable marriage', despite the fact that Edwin has had the good sense to leave the cage door open. This symbolic image closes Chapter Four of Book Four, a formal structuring which serves to emphasise the finality of Julia's situation.

All three sisters show solidarity with each other, at least until Julia's failed love affair and subsequent marriage distance her from the others. Emmy and Lisbet, however, support each other emotionally and physically to the end. One of the most moving episodes in the novel is Lisbet's frantic retracing of Emmy's journey through the storm in her doomed attempt to elope with Stephen, a formal device which is necessary because of the first person narrative form, but one which allows the reader to experience Emmy's original panic-stricken flight without the danger of melodrama while it simultaneously confirms the bond between the sisters. There is no such bond between mother and daughters. The mother is on the periphery of the action here and when she does move closer to centre stage, she seems oblivious of her husband's domineering ways or of the danger represented by his locum Mr Boyd, whose unwelcome sexual attentions Emmy describes imagistically and powerfully 'as though some one had lifted a flap of the carpet and filled my nose with dust' (129). Ultimately, however, the 'absence' of the mother speaks as eloquently of the unmanageability of the female role as do the overt disasters which befall her daughters and again it is the imagery of the poetic narrative which speaks for her. Lisbet comes upon her sitting alone in the parlour:

> pleating her sewing between her fingers to crease it into a hem while she remarked what a pity it was papa was always so unreasonable when he was ill. Suddenly I wondered what she really thought within herself, what ships sailed into her harbour when she sat alone (115).

As in the breakfast table scene in Book One Chapter One, Lisbet's momentary insight makes manifest the empty life of a mother whose youthful vitality has been vanquished by external forces beyond her control and who cannot now provide an acceptable role model or authority figure in adult life for her daughters. She is as imprisoned as they are within the social conventions of the time.

So far, this essay has been concerned with the imagistic nature of the *The Gowk Storm* narrative. Another related linguistic element which is of interest for the subtext it conveys is the Scots dialect spoken by certain of the characters. In contrast to the use of Scots by nineteenth-century novelists such as Scott, Hogg and Stevenson to indicate positive or characterful qualities in rural or lower-class figures, in *The Gowk Storm* Scots-speaking characters are on the whole malicious, prejudiced, superstitious and working against any change towards a freer, less life-denying system of social values. There are minor exceptions: the toll man who helps Lisbet search for Emmy and the coachman who comes to break the news to Edwin of his daughter's drowning. But in general a negative resonance is found with Scots-speaking characters such as the petty-minded, vicious church elders who drive the Catholic schoolmaster from his charge; the apparently friendly, gossiping Mrs Wands whose house is always open to visitors, but whose careless tongue and superstitious nature provide ammunition for those who wish to despatch the dominie; and, perhaps surprisingly, Nannie, the old nurse and general servant who acts as a mother-substitute for the girls. Nannie's proverbial sayings and sharp, couthy Scots tongue may appear to represent her in the traditional manner as a strong, colourful character; in actuality they close down opportunities for the discussion of difficulties and therefore for any attempt to question or modify oppressive situations. 'Do you believe, Nannie . . . in leaving everything with God, or do you think we should make efforts to change things?' (92), Emmy asks, as the girls sit in the kitchen after the departure of the dominie, whose own unwillingness to fight for Julia, his being, as she had chided, 'so sure of defeat he never went into battle' (61), has demonstrated male power over women as surely as has the prohibition of her father. Nanny, however, will have nothing to do with Emmy's suggestion that at this late stage of human development people should perhaps attempt to influence what happens in their lives:

> 'God's will is as clear noo as it was then', Nannie said finally, 'but mebbe we are no so clear aboot looking for it whit wi' always wanting whit we havena been gi'en. Ye can do withoot so muckle ye ne'er thocht ye could – ye can do withoot almost anything' (92–3).

This is a philosophy of endurance, understandable, perhaps, on the part of an old woman who has spent her life at the beck and call of others, with no opportunity for individual self-fulfilment. It is also, however, a philosophy which works against any possibility of change.

Finally, I would like to return to Virginia Woolf's comment about the capacity of poetry in fiction to open up wider questions of destiny and the meaning of life. Early in the narrative we are presented with two opposing philosophical responses to life in the values of Julia and her schoolmaster lover. For the dominie, as for Nannie, 'this life is given us to find out how much we can do without', a view which provokes the response from Julia: 'Nonsense . . . we are here to enjoy, to have and to share, not to deny and chill ourselves' (32). These two comments, the dominie's negative philosophy and Julia's more positive, even hedonistic one, could almost be epigraphs to the novel, raising as they do questions about the interpretation we place on human life: whether it is for fulfilment or for the endurance of suffering; whether we fight for what we believe in or accept that change is outwith our control. Lisbet's elegiac narrative raises equally significant questions about the nature of human existence *per se* in relation to the physical universe. When the sisters spend ten days together at St Andrews before Julia's marriage, Lisbet watches the 'sweep of sky joining the sea at the pale horizon' and thinks, in a cosmic image reminiscent of MacDiarmid's poetry 'of the earth after millions of years when life has left it, like a shell worn with holes, filled only with windy vibrations: the faint echo of the sea, the whisper of spent rain, a weak sighing as of prayer' (98). One is reminded of the opening description of the sky and mountains in Book One, Chapter One, where the world seemed to have 'resolved itself again into the contours and substances that composed it before man trod on its earth and drank in its air' (7) or Lisbet's description of the schoolchidren who gave her 'the uneasy impression of mites gambolling at the foot of an unseeing eternity' (69).

As we have seen, despite its manse setting, institutionalised religion is not presented positively in this novel, its practitioners and its doctrines characterised as hostile to life-enhancing qualities. Similarly, the closing image of the Barnfingal graveyard as described by Lisbet subverts traditional Christian symbolism of resurrection 'with its grey gravestones all *blankly* facing east' (178) [my italics]. Instead, in this ending, we are left with her evocation of the cry of the curlew: '[a]ll the world's sorrow, all the world's pain, and none of its regret, lay throbbing in that cry' (178). As in the cosmic images referred to earlier, there is an impersonality in this image which communicates a view of human life as transient and insignificant in relation to the determined pattern of an indifferent physical universe, not the chosen centrepiece of God's creation as in traditional Christian teaching – an unsettling perspective on human life which scientific discoveries were increasingly forcing to the front of the religious debate in the later nineteenth and early twentieth centuries. Yet opposing this bleak philosophical perspective is the message communicated through the imagery of the narrative that, in the human timespan we inherit, we can and should make the most of our transient lives. Through the implications of its poetic narrative, Nancy Brysson Morrison's novel is therefore not only a plea that the social conditions under which women live their lives should be remedied so that they can have some control over these lives; it is also a plea for human beings, men and women, to respond with all their vitality to the living moment in a life which in its wider philosophical context is fleeting and beyond human control.

Works Cited

Carswell, Catherine *Open the Door!*. 1920; Edinburgh: Canongate, 1986

Gilbert, Sandra M. and Susan Gubar eds. *Shakespeare's Sisters: Feminist Essays on Women Poets*. Bloomington: Indiana University Press, 1979

Grigson, Geoffrey ed. *The Penguin Book of Ballads*. Harmondsworth: Penguin Books, 1975

Macherey, Pierre *A Theory of Literary Production*. G.Wall trans. 1966; London: Routledge, 1978

Morrison, Nancy Brysson *The Gowk Storm*. 1933; Edinburgh: Canongate, 1988

Woolf, Virginia 'Women and Fiction' in *Women and Writing*. Michèle Barrett intro. London: The Women's Press, 1979

Jessie Kesson (1916–94)

Jessie Kesson was born Jessie Grant McDonald in the Workhouse at Inverness on the seventeenth of November 1916. She was the illegitimate daughter of Elizabeth McDonald, whose father never forgave this disgrace. She was brought up in poverty until the age of eight in an Elgin slum, where her mother led an unconventional sex life. Jessie loved her mother deeply, and learned her love of poetry from her.

But eventually the Court removed her from her mother's care, to a small orphanage in Skene, Aberdeenshire, where she did well at school, encouraged by a fine Dominie, who encouraged her to aspire to university education. But the orphanage Trustees considered education wasted on a girl, and she was put out to domestic service on a local farm. The frustrated aspiring writer had a breakdown, and spent a year in a mental hospital, before being boarded out at Abriachan, north of Loch Ness. There she met and married Johnny Kesson, and after three years on Skye they returned to the North-east and spent years cottaring on farms, with long hours, tied houses, and the fear of 'the sack without words'. They had two children, Avril and Kenneth, and Jessie began her incredible joint careers as worker, mother *and* writer.

Encouraged by a chance encounter with writer Nan Shepherd, she blossomed into print, and then into radio, where she became perhaps the finest Scottish writer in the 'golden age of Scottish broadcasting', 1947–55. Meanwhile they moved to London, where Jessie had a bizarre series of jobs; cleaning nurses' quarters at Colney Hatch Mental Hospital; Saturdays in Woolworths; cinema cleaner; cook; social worker; and running educational courses and old folks' homes. Her favourite job, except for some happy months as a producer for Woman's Hour, was as a life model; being paid, as she said, for thinking her own thoughts. She also spent a few years at East Linton working with disturbed teenagers, after Johnny retired.

And all this time she was wife and mother, and writing radio plays for the BBC in Aberdeen, Glasgow and Edinburgh, for the Third Programme, for the Home Service (Radio Four), and latterly for television. At intervals she published the four slim volumes for which she is still best known; *The*

White Bird Passes in 1958; *Glitter of Mica* in 1963; *Another Time, Another Place* in 1983, and *Where the Apple Ripens* (short stories) in 1985. In 1980 Mike Radford made a BBC film of *The White Bird Passes*, followed by an interview with the author, which brought her a belated general recognition, and later she and Mike Radford collaborated on the film *Another Time, Another Place* – while she simultaneously wrote the novel: she had originally written it as a radio play – and it won international recognition in a shower of prizes.

But Johnny, some twelve years her senior, had poor health, and increasingly Jessie was torn between public demands on her time, and students' requests for help with dissertations, and her need to care for him, as she herself developed angina and became too easily tired. Johnny died at last in August 1994, and Jessie succumbed to lung cancer after many years of smoking which contributed to her wonderful husky Doric voice, dying on the twenty-eighth of October that same year.

Isobel Murray

Borderlines: Jessie Kesson's
The White Bird Passes

Glenda Norquay

In interviews Jessie Kesson emerges as a lively and down-to-earth figure, a woman who made no secret of the fact that her own origins were to a large extent the basis for *The White Bird Passes*. This evident link between her experience and her writing, and the connections which can be made between her own, well-recorded, vibrant voice and the vivid folk 'speak' of her narrative style, have all contributed to the critical perspective in which she has been viewed. Roderick Watson is one of several critics who have placed her work in the tradition of north-east writing, with its strong strain of 'vivid sentimental realism' (Watson 1984, 394), a comment echoed in Cuthbert Graham's assertion that '*The White Bird Passes* is social comment. It belongs, in fact, to the long succession of north-east fictions of radical realism' (Graham, 1980, 4). Isobel Murray also stresses the 'confessional' aspect of her writing, although emphasising the strategic nature of this autobiographical slant: 'She had to create herself and tell her own story, defining herself as best as she could: this is what made *The White Bird Passes* in particular such an urgent and demanding task' (Murray, 1995, 183). However, the appeal of reading her work in autobiographical terms, and of placing her in a particular generic and regional context, should not blind us to the complexities of her work, to the craft of *The White Bird Passes* and its subtly paradigmatic structure. The novel maps out a pattern of female development but also offers a model for understanding the growth of a class and gendered identity which moves beyond the specifics of experience it details.

The White Bird Passes traces the early years of a young girl, Janie, growing up in the north-east of Scotland, brought up in backstreet poverty by her mother, Liza. It follows her removal by the authorities from that lively but precarious world, her transfer to an orphanage, and her emergence into a new world of adult sexuality and the ambiguous possibility of escape through education. In many ways, then, *The White Bird Passes* would appear to be the novel of a 'lass o' pairts'. What sets it apart from the Kailyard tradition, however, is not just its delineation of poverty and degradation but its celebration of border communities and its exploration of the boundaries which construct social, psychic and sexual identity. The novel can be read as an extended metaphor for women's troubled and marginalised position within the symbolic order, following as it does the development of Janie, who although the central character seems to be always positioned upon the edge, whether of family life, social structures and of sexual identity, and mapping out the different worlds she inhabits. In this essay I want to suggest that the striking characteristic of *The White Bird Passes* is the way in which a fairly conventional trajectory of development into adulthood is placed against a wider delineation of those structures of power which define the social. The novel traces out the pattern of Janie's youth but, through its focus on the margins, also examines, questions and subverts the constituents of the world into which she is growing.

The White Bird Passes is, then, a novel which follows a central character crossing the border from childhood to adulthood and examines the tensions and conflicts of that development. But it is also a novel which explores the borders between different worlds, different social groups and ways of living. 'Borderlines' in the novel can therefore be traced in both its chronological developments and its social and psychic topography, as the opening chapter demonstrates. The novel begins with Janie as a figure moving along a boundary: running through Lady's Lane. This street where she lives, now the poorest area of town, takes its name from Our Lady and the monks who once used it. Possessed of an ancient, dignified, and masculine history, it is now the domain of fierce female grotesques who watch Janie's every movement and control her day:

> If you rushed down High Street in a hurry, you wouldn't notice Lady's Lane at all, so narrowly and darkly does it skulk itself away, but Lady's Lane would most certainly see you. At all hours of the day a voluntary look-out lounges against the entrance to the Lane. It may be Poll Pyke, Battleaxe or the Duchess. For those ladies of the Lane are in some mysterious way self–appointed guardians of the Lane (1–2).

These powerful figures, known to the reader only by the nicknames Janie and everyone else gives them, offer a reinscription of Lady's Lane, and provide its character. Although hidden from the respectable world of the High Street, and in that sense occupying a marginal position, they are not peripheral within their own world, but remain its controlling forces. And it is in relation to these figures that Janie is first identified and understood. We watch her being asked to perform errands for each of the Lane's idiosyncratic figures, a series of tasks revolving around either food or sex. And in each instance the women give Janie something in return: Annie Frigg furnishes a world of imagination, in her promises of exotic presents which never materialise; Mysie Walsh, the prostitute, with her warm arms, scents and songs, offers a special kind of affection; even the Duchess bestows the approval of a matriarch. These very different women contribute to providing points of definition for Janie's emerging identity.

Positioned behind the High Street, the Lane however also offers a defining point for the social order: it stands for that which must be controlled from the outside by masculine representatives of authority – the Sanitary Man, the Cruelty Inspector, the Free Boot Man. A world whose borders are policed and strictly demarcated, its internal preoccupations are with sexuality, survival, food, gossip, and street spectacle – whether of women fighting, children playing games, or the body of Mysie Walsh, who has committed suicide, being taken away. The Lane is also the source for a range of vibrant Scottish voices, songs and tales. Together these elements make it appear as an unruly human body, representative of a threat to order, probity and respectability which must be constrained and confined. The defining point of Janie's identity, home to the women who play an important part in her development, it also offers a symbolic representation of the referents of her own particular world.

Although this world is policed by figures of patriarchal authority, it is female role models and surrogate mothers who dominate the early chapters of the story – much more so than Janie's own mother, Liza, who is not introduced until halfway through the second chapter, and then only briefly. These alternative mothers figure largely in Janie's developing sense of herself and of her world, and contributing to our understanding of her vulnerable position on the edges of conventional family structures. Liza is presented in the novel as a complex and enigmatic figure, of considerable importance to Janie but less reliable in her moods and fancies than other women in the Lane, and of higher social origins. For Janie, as for most daughters, the maternal space is a problematic one: 'If Janie had been suddenly stricken with blindness she would have had a perpetual picture of her Mother in her memory. Not a photograph. Her Mother had so many faces. But a hundred little images. Each of which was some part of her Mother. And her Mother some part of each.'(16). So, while Janie may search through her mother for a sense of unitary wholeness, her mother is composed for her only of fragments. Her mother also occupies an outcast position socially: her own family is a respectable rural one but, it is implied, because of her illegitimate child, she has been cast out from them and no longer acknowledged by her father although her mother maintains a link with both daughter and granddaughter. A further area of tension for Janie as a child is her mother's troubling sexuality, and the way in which she exploits this to make a living for them.

Her family background appears even more problematic for Janie because of the absence of a father. She desires a protective figure like her friend Gertie's father, 'Gertie didn't know what it was to sneck the door and hide under the bed when they came. Her Dad was there to attack the attacker, shouting right down the Lane after him . . . '(33) and fabricates a dead father out of her imagination, a father who loved the tin whistle, but the only surrogate fathers she encounters are those figures of male authority of whom she is afraid: the Cruelty Man, the Free Boot Man, the Sanitary Man. Yet while she may long for a strong father, indulging in a fantasy in which, to the astonishment of the rest of the class, the school Headmaster reveals himself to be her father, the absence of such a figure may not be as great a loss as she believes. For Janie to make a full transition into the symbolic order, and a world of conventional gender roles, a recognition of patriarchal power is necessary; yet for a large part of the novel there is no such figure to complete this process on a personal, rather than institutional level. So, until she encounters 'the Mannie', who helps run the Orphanage, oppressive power and patriarchy are always quite explicitly linked in her mind. 'The Mannie', moreover, is a figure of gentleness, associated with nature, with a world out of doors, and of less obvious authority than his wife. He may function in acknowledging Janie's awakening sexuality, but plays little part in directing her future. As a result when Janie does move into the adult world it is very much on her own terms: the lack of a father may, in a symbolic sense, make it easier for her to refuse conventional gender oppositions.

Rather than this unconventional upbringing and family context being presented only as disabling, it gives Janie a position on the edges of the symbolic order, providing an education and culture of a different kind. This alternative perspective applies in class as well as gender terms: economically and socially Janie appears at home on the edges of society. Indeed, she is shown (when a child) as being more at ease in this world than her mother: it is Janie who becomes friends with Beulah, the tinker who lives on the

Green; it is Janie who responds with enthusiasm to a night in the Diddle Doddle – the itinerants' boarding-house. Her awareness of a range of different worlds, each with their own sets of hierarchies, but also with their own rich strangeness, thus allows Janie to maintain a certain separateness from authority. When they flee the authorities and end up spending the night in the Diddle Doddle, Janie, unlike her mother, is enchanted by its colour, life and variety of types. Later she advises a friend in the Children's Home to imagine figures of authority without their clothes, in order to subvert their power. This awareness of and attraction to the comic grotesque is a powerful factor in defining Janie's identity just as the life, the colour, and drama, as well as the poverty, dirt and fighting, of the Lane give her a particular imaginative creativity. When finally separated from her mother and told that she will be taken to the orphanage at Skeyne, she immediately thinks of the word 'skein', and the way in which the Duchess, who was always busy crocheting a blanket, would run out of the brightly coloured threads and search for a new skein:

> There was some magical quality to the Duchess's bright bed-cover. You felt it would never come to an end and turn into a real bed-cover. And all because of some elusive skein. Skeyne. Janie liked the sound of the place where the Home was (102).

The peripheral worlds of the text thus supply an imaginative richness, which undermines the discourses of authority, and it is the influence of these worlds which determines Janie's character and development.

Borderline worlds and the idea of the grotesque thus perform complex roles in the novel, questioning and exposing the structures of power. In *The Politics and Poetics of Transgression* Peter Stallybrass and Allon White define Bakhtin's concept of grotesque realism as follows:

> Grotesque realism uses the material body – flesh conceptualized as corpulent excess – to represent cosmic, social topographical and linguistic elements of the world. Thus already in Bakhtin there is the germinal notion of transcodings and displacements effected between the low/high image of the physical body and other social domains (Stallybrass and White, 1986, 8–9).

As an example they cite the occupation of Greenham Common by women, the creation of a marginal world which revealed 'how the grotesque body may become a primary, highly-charged intersection and mediation of social and political forces, a sort of intensifier and displacer in the making of identity'(25). This concept of a marginal world of the grotesque, which because of its marginality offers a powerful symbolic domain both intensifying and displacing constructions of identity, can – as indicated – be applied to the unruly world of the Lane but also illuminates the significance of two other locations within the novel: the Green and the Diddle Doddle.

The Lane is bordered by the Green which is, even in a literal sense, the space of the Carnivalesque: it is occupied for a time by the circus, then by the fair, and finally, by the tinkers:

> The Green had its own social scale. Lord John Sanger's circus was the cream of its aristocracy. When the circus arrived, the chair-o-planes, the Strong Man, the coconut stalls, withdrew from the centre of the Green and huddled themselves away in a more remote direction, like younger sons knowing their proper place but still dependent. When winter came and the last circus elephant had trumpeted its way to the station, and the show's last caravan rumbled along the North Road, leaving only faded, brown circles on the Green's grass to prove that they had ever been there at all, the tinkers, the third and last grade of the Green's society, took over (39–40).

Bakhtin claimed for the carnivalesque in a medieval context 'a sense of the gay relativity of prevailing truths and authorities' (Morris, 1994, 200). In the changing hierarchies of peripheral worlds, instability and relativity function as a means of questioning hierarchies in the core world: 'We find here a characteristic logic, the peculiar logic of the 'inside out' (*à l'envers*), of the 'turnabout', of a continual shifting from top to bottom, from front to rear, of numerous parodies and travesties, humiliations, profanations, comic crownings and uncrownings' (Morris, 200). This concept of 'turnabout' could be seen as a description of the novel's narrative strategy as it works through a series of juxtaposed peripheral worlds whose hierarchies both imitate and undermine the authority of the social order. In each of the worlds Janie meets new figures of apparent authority, whose claim to power is then reversed or inverted – Poll Pyke and Battleaxe fight in the streets for their status; Beulah, initially a role model for Janie is revealed as a conwoman; even the Duchess is demoted from her position of power by moving out of the Lane and into a new council house. Later in the novel Mrs Thane runs the Orphanage with absolute power, until the governors arrive and she must defer to them. These various Queen figures rule over their particular domains but only for a limited period. And yet each of their domains serves to undermine the idea of a secure and effective central authority.

This sense of transitory worlds and shifting hierarchies is also brought out in allusions to the networks of fairs and travellers, which Janie longs to be part of. In this liminal world the reader, like Janie, is exposed to the litany of names and places, markets and fairs, which have already acquired a glamorous quality in her conversations with Beulah:

> But the tinkers also had the magical facility of rolling far-sounding places round their tongues.
>
> Aikey Fair, 'Where the ale cost only tuppence and a tanner bocht a gill.' Raffan Market, its horse sales with brown, furtive tinkers 'wheezing gajes for jowldie' – taking country men for suckers. Blairgowrie, the great trek southwards to the berry-picking, and 'I'll show ye the road and the miles to Dundee, Janie' (40).

The sense of being on the road, of being part of a network of marginal communities, whose people traverse 'ordinary' spaces to reach extraordinary but transitory destinations, offers a powerful alternative image to the fixed institutional world which seeks to contain Janie.

Certain characteristics of the carnival world are also drawn upon to question the relationship between economies of work and pleasure in the novel. Stallybrass and White describe the fair as a place 'structured by the juxtaposition of the domestic and the bizarre, the local and the exotic' (39) – it is a space which blurs pleasure and business, amusement and trading. Beulah, with her poaching, her trading of rags, and her reminiscences of past fairs and markets, clearly offers a similar confusion of categories. The Lane would seem to contain a similar blurring of boundaries, in particular through the romantic image of prostitution. Certainly it does so in the case of Mysie, who is presented as making money from her natural sensuality rather than selling her body. Even Liza refuses the man who has brought her home, throwing his money away because he sees their relationship only as a 'business deal'. Yet in his transatlantic language the rejected client points towards a newer world in which sex is seen purely as a commodity: 'What about my dough? I paid you, didn't I?'(25). The Lane, too, is undergoing a transition, as differences emerge between those who work at home – the women who guard the alley – and those who go out to work for others. When millworkers come clattering up the Lane its 'Ladies' are dispossessed:

The Duchess and her coterie diminished on Thursday night, leaning against the causeway with silent disapproval while the Lane's up-and-coming race held the cobbles and, even more galling, held them in an idiom alien to her Grace; flaunting overmuch of that tin jewellery from Woolworth's, that new store, Nothing Over Sixpence, that had just opened in High Street . . . '(10).

These newcomers are part of a world of commodity circulation, earning their money in the mill, spending it in stores, and drawing sharp distinctions between labour and pleasure. Much later in the novel, when Janie is taken into the orphanage, her daily occupations point towards a similar process of categorisation, for the Home is a world graded by tasks, ranked according to their unpleasantness: the youngest has to sweep leaves in the yard, move up to cleaning boots, and so on until at the end of the novel Janie has the desirable job of delivering milk. The institution thus controls the relationship between work and pleasure. In this context there is a certain ambiguity about Janie's future occupation. If she were to reject the options on offer – maid or farmworker – and find a means of combining pleasure and labour in education, she would' be subverting that institutional control. Yet in so doing she would ironically be leaving the margins behind and moving into the centre.

The third aspect of Bakhtin's ideas on carnival which can be applied to the novel is a linguistic one. He writes: 'The familiar language of the marketplace became a reservoir in which various speech patterns excluded from official discourse could freely accumulate' (Morris, 204). While *The White Bird Passes* tends to place all its abusive and profane language in the mouths of certain characters, it also works through juxtaposition of different and conflicting forms of discourse. The epigraph to the novel is taken from Stevenson's *Songs of Travel* (XIV): '*Bright is the ring of words*', and the novel creates a ring of voices and words through its range of verse and song, interleaved through the text. Some are from Scottish folk-songs, children's street songs, other from hymns, yet more from popular songs of the period, including American minstrel vernacular. It is only towards the close of the novel that the voice of a more authoritative high culture emerges and even here it is in an ambiguous context. Janie draws upon Shelley when thinking of her mother and her mother's death, and uses the lines from *The Tempest* – '*Of his bones are coral made*' – as a way of stopping herself laughing when confronted with the panel who will decide her future after leaving the Orphanage (142). The opposition of high and low voices is clear, as high culture enables her to suppress damaging, excessive and subversive

laughter. In contrast the 'low' of popular culture would seem to point towards recognised links between very different 'marginal' communities as
the children sing in the street: '*We're two little piccanninies*' (90). While it
is possible to see the novel as moving towards a greater engagement with
the language of high culture, Scots is still the language of the body at its
close. Even when Janie has gained much greater access to education, it is
the lines sung by the Mannie which evoke her awakening sexuality, '*For
Nancy's hair is yella like gowd*' and '*O my lass, ye'll get a man*' (132).

Moreover, if the novel draws upon a range of discourses in its narrative,
Janie's perspective is conveyed through a voice that, while not quite the folk
voice of *A Scots Quair*, still draws heavily on her own culture:

> And he should know, Janie thought, watching him curiously, for he
> had cut down the corpse. He has seen somebody dead. She stared at
> his face to find the imprint so strange a seeing must have left upon
> it. His face looked the same as it always did in his dark, cobbler's
> shop, his eyes pale and peering, with yellow stuff stuck in the corners'
> (*29–30*).

Here the increased colloquialism imitates Janie's attempt to make the strange
seem familiar. In contrast, a more Latinate construction can suggest a perspective somewhat more adult than Janie's, and express an engagement
with authority, as when Janie and Liza are contemplating separation and
the Orphanage:

> Liza's voice increased the desolation of those last moments together.
> The anteroom smelt sharp and clinical as all Janie's preconceived ideas
> of 'a Home'. Its austerity more fearful than any pool of blood that
> had ever incarnadined the Lane. Its silence more ominous than all the
> curses coursing through the causeway' (100).

And yet, while Janie may appear to be moving into the established social
order at the novel's close, the final words belong more to the world of dialect,
of Scots, and of disorder as the Mannie calls the children back to the home:
'Janie! O, there ye are! Where are the ithers? Chris! Alice! Donnie! Come on
in, now. Come on! The hale jing bang o' ye! Come on awa' in . . . ' (p.153).
The semantics are an attempt to impose control, but the words themselves,
especially the glorious 'hale jing bang', ring out as a celebration of disorder.

It is, however, through the idea of the body itself that the novel most
clearly problematises the connections between worlds of marginality and

Janie's entry into the sexual and social: here, more than anywhere else, the grotesque is used as a way of exploring boundaries. For Janie, brought up by a mother whose sexual life has become a determining factor in her identity – through her illegitimate child, her reputation for a certain promiscuity and through her fatal syphilis – and emerging into adult sexuality herself by the end of the novel, awareness of her own body is clearly significant. As a child we are given detailed descriptions of how her clothes fell; at the close of the novel her body is awakening to the glances and desires of the men around her. But the novel also makes the reader alert to the boundaries of the body through its focus on deformity. The Diddle Doddle in which Janie and her mother take refuge is the temporary home of tinkers and other itinerants: as such it gives shelter to a range of 'freaks'. Here they encounter a man with no legs but with a 'great, black hairy grin' (96); Blind Jimmy – a wonderful singer but 'a bit too free with his hands the moment he gets within an inch of a woman' (97); a Fortune Teller and a poacher. The uneasy combination of deformity and sexuality, licence and law-breaking, both frightens and enthrals but drives her mother back into the arms of authority. As Mary Russo notes in *The Female Grotesque: Risk, Excess and Modernity*: 'The grotesque body was exuberantly and democratically open and inclusive of all possibilities. Boundaries between individuals and society, between genders, between species, and between classes, were blurred or brought into crisis in the inversions and hyperbole of the carnivalesque' (Russo, 1994, 78). The people in the Diddle Doddle, occupying a space on the borders of the community and with their own idiosyncratic shapes, call into question categorisation of both the physical and social body. Thus the troubled area of female sexuality can best be mapped out in relation to the carnival grotesque, which serves to question boundaries both of the body and of sexual convention.

This essay began by attempting to move away from too close an identification of Kesson's own experiences with the narrative concerns of *The White Bird Passes*, and has attempted to show the way in which Kesson's work can be understood in terms of the Carnivalesque and the grotesque. Kesson herself, however, offered just such a reading of her writing; it seems only fitting that her voice, in its very language resistant to the centre, should have the last word. In a 1985 interview with Isobel Murray she sums up her theme:

But I realised myself what I was writing aboot. At long last . . . And I thocht, that's it, that's really what everything I've written is aboot – *queer* fowk! . . . 'Queer fowk, who are oot, and niver hiv ony desire

to be in!' . . . Every work I've ever written contains ae 'ootlin'. Lovely
Aberdeenshire word. Somebody that never really fitted into the thing
(Murray, 1996, 58; Kesson slightly misquotes her own novel here; see
The White Bird Passes, 112).

It is through Kesson's fascination with 'ootlins', with the marginal, that the
novel's powerful critique of the centre emerges. In her narrative she has
created a style which alerts us to hierarchies of discourse and to cultural
borderlines. By encouraging us to focus on the borders of the body, the
boundaries between work and pleasure, and borderlines between different
social worlds, she leads us into a questioning of demarcations of gender
and class. In each instance the margins are used to interrogate the centre.
In the novel Janie's Aunt Morag has a box of 'magic treasures', special
objects collected over the years, with which she taunts Janie, letting the
child look at all the flashing beads, bright bottles and brooches but then
closing the box without giving her anything. The contents of the box,
however, cannot be contained: even with the lid shut they spill over into
Janie's imagination and live there. Likewise, as we follow Janie's development we may see her moving towards the centre, into the social order, but
it is the words and worlds of the 'ootlin' that remain vivid in the reader's
mind.

Works Cited

Graham, Cuthbert 'Introduction' to *The White Bird Passes*. Edinburgh: Paul
    Harris, 1980
Hendry, Joy 'Jessie Kesson's White Bird', *Chapman*. No. 27–8. Summer
    1980, 122–4
Hendry, Joy Jessie Kesson Country, *The Scots Magazine*. 132. October
    1989, 11–22
Hewitt, David ed. *Northern Visions: Essays on the Literary Identity of
    Northern Scotland in the Twentieth Century*. East Linton: Tuckwell Press,
    1995
Kesson, Jessie *The White Bird Passes*. 1958; Edinburgh: B & W Publishing,
    1996
Morris, Pam ed. *The Bakhtin Reader: Selected Writings of Bakhtin,
    Medvedev, Voloshinov*. London: Edward Arnold, 1994 (References in
    particular to excerpts from *Rabelais and His World*, 1965, 195–206)

Murray Isobel ed. 'The Sma' Perfect: Jessie Kesson' in *Scottish Writers Talking: Interviewed by Isobel Murray and Bob Tait*. East Linton: Tuckwell Press, 1996, 55–83

Murray, Isobel 'Jessie Kesson: Writing Herself', in Hewitt (above), 180–189

Russo, Mary *The Female Grotesque: Risk, Excess and Modernity*. London: Routledge, 1994

Stallybrass, Peter and Allon White *The Politics and Poetics of Transgression*. London: Methuen, 1986

Watson, Roderick *The Literature of Scotland*. London: Macmillan, 1984

Muriel Spark (b.1918)

Muriel Spark was born in 1918 in Edinburgh, daughter of Bernard Camberg, Edinburgh-Jewish and an engineer, and Sarah Uezzell from Hertfordshire; Spark was educated at James Gillespie's School for Girls, across the links at Bruntsfield from where her family lived, and, briefly, Heriot Watt College. She left Edinburgh in 1937 for Rhodesia (Zimbabwe) to marry Oswald Spark. She had one son, Robin; separated from her husband, Spark returned to England, 1944, where she worked in the political intelligence department of the Foreign Office. She was secretary of the Poetry Society, 1947–49, and edited *Poetry Review*; she wrote or edited various works on the Brontes, Mary Shelley, John Masefield, John Henry Newman and others. She won *The Observer* short story competition in 1951 with her first short story 'The Seraph and the Zambezi'. She converted to Roman Catholicism in 1954. Her first novel was *The Comforters* (1957), *The Ballad of Peckham Rye* (1960) was her fourth, *The Prime of Miss Jean Brodie* (1961) her sixth; her thirteen subsequent novels have included *A Far Cry from Kensington* (1988), *Symposium* (1990) and *Reality and Dreams* (1996); both her poems and her short stories have been collected; her autobiography *Curriculum Vitae* (1992) covers her life up to the publication of her first novel. She left London in 1962, living first in New York, and then, from 1966, in Italy where she still lives. She has received many literary prizes and honours and was made a Dame of the British Empire in 1994.

A.C.

Certainty and Unease in Muriel Spark's *The Ballad of Peckham Rye*

Aileen Christianson

Muriel Spark is often seen by non-Scottish critics as a postmodern writer, someone who is part of 'English' literature, rather than as specifically a woman writer or a Scottish writer. Her idiosyncratic concerns are defined by critics as Sparkian rather than feminist or Scottish. Indeed there is an evenhandedness about her approach to gender in her novels, as there is to class: women and men are equally satirised, weaknesses exposed, social position and gender differences categorised. Her fictional world is concerned with morality, with reality and illusion, with the simultaneity of the natural and the supernatural. She has explicitly separated herself from women writers: 'When I started writing, there was a lot of timid writing especially by women. I hope that's finished' (*Ex-S*, 29 Jan. 96) but has embraced her Scottishness; speaking of her early belief that women were equal to men, she has said:

> 'I thought feminism was a thing of the past. My grandmother was a Suffragette, she marched for the vote. I thought it was over. I was born free, being a Scot'. (A mischievous glance here, but she confirmed this later, that she was *Scottish*, her English mother, Jewish father and predisposition to Rome notwithstanding) (Jenkins' interview, 1988).

The absolutism of the Calvinist God and the Jewish God of the Old Testament combine in the fearsome control that Spark exercises over her novels. Her narrators are authoritarian, and the author behind them, far from being dead, is insistent in interview and in her autobiography, *Curriculum Vitae*

(1990), on her conscious awareness both of the autobiographical roots of much of her writing and the skill that renders that material into her concise and un–autobiographical works. The continuing problem for any Spark criticism is that her control of her material is so total, the brevity disguising an intricately patterned, layered narrative where every interpretation is covered and allowed for by the authorial providence which is as authoritarian, though more mischievous, than the God of Calvin.[1] What remains for the critic is the disentanglement of the compressed density of her fiction.

In this essay she will be examined as someone who, despite exile, despite setting nearly all of her fiction outwith Scotland, still writes from within Scottish traditions as seen in the ballads, in Hogg's *Confessions of a Justified Sinner*, in R. L. Stevenson's *Dr Jekyll and Mr Hyde*, exploring themes of betrayal, sudden death, duality, and displaying absolute acceptance of fantastic as well as realistic worlds, with an unforgiving God and an infinitely changeable devil. She is clear herself that her upbringing and education in Edinburgh had an ineradicable effect on her ways of thinking and writing. 'My religious education at school had been Presbyterian for which, with its predominant accent on the lovely Bible, I have always been grateful' (*Curriculum Vitae* 116). The absolute nature of the God of Calvin who 'sees the beginning and the end' that Sandy sees hovering behind Jean Brodie's actions in *The Prime of Miss Jean Brodie* (1961, 120), had been inculcated in Spark at school, in conjunction with rather than in opposition to her family's Jewishness. 'We were fed the Border Ballads and the Old Testament, and they had a huge influence. All that sudden death, no weeping over the grave. Death is death: that struck me early in life' (Jenkins' interview, 1988). She writes of 'reading the Border ballads so repetitively and attentively that I memorised many of them without my noticing it. The steel and bite of the ballads, so remorseless and yet so lyrical, entered my literary bloodstream never to depart' (*Curriculum Vitae* 98). In 'How I became a Novelist', still thinking of herself as essentially a poet, Spark said of *The Ballad of Peckham Rye*, published in early 1960, that she wanted to give her 'mind a holiday and to write something light and lyrical – as near a poem as a novel could get, and in as few words as possible' (1960, 683). Thus she presents it as inevitable that her style and themes should echo the ballads and that the lyrical brevity she sought in writing the *Ballad* was already ingrained in her, believing, as she wrote later, that the 'novel as an art form was essentially an extension of poetry' (*Curriculum Vitae* 206). The essential Spark style was to rest on brevity and clarity.

'Fiction to me is a kind of parable. You have got to make up your mind it's not true. Some kind of truth emerges from it, but it's not fact'

('My Conversion', 1961, 63). Thus Spark begins her interrogation of the nature of fiction, aligning herself with the medieval view of the function of literature. This is the assumption that literature is not simply mimetic of reality, but that layered interpretations are to be expected as discernible in any text. She was more explicit in her 1962 interview with Frank Kermode:

> I don't claim that my novels are truth – I claim that they are fiction, out of which a kind of truth emerges. And I keep in my mind specifically that what I am writing is fiction because I am interested in truth – absolute truth – and I don't pretend that what I'm writing is more than an imaginative extension of the truth – something inventive.... There is metaphorical truth and moral truth, and what they call anagogical ... and there is absolute truth, in which I believe things which are difficult to believe, but I believe them because they are absolute. And this is one aspect of truth, perhaps. But in fact if we are going to live in the world as reasonable beings, we must call it lies ('House of Fiction', 133).

Implicit in this is the certainty of layers of meaning relating directly to medieval formulations of literary interpretations: the story at a literal level, the allegorical or metaphorical meaning, the moral or tropological meaning, and finally the anagogical level leading to the absolute truths that only God can really know, to which we can only aspire. It places Spark's fictions in the context of a moral interpretation, of parable, their surface accessible and entertaining, but containing behind that possibilities for complex interpretative layers of meaning. Dougal Douglas's spoof sociologist's 'four types of morality observable in Peckham.... One, emotional. Two, functional. Three, puritanical. Four, Christian' (*Ballad* 83) are an allusion to this kind of layered interpretation, the layers of meaning intermingled, as are Dougal's 'moral categories': 'Sometimes all are to be found in the beliefs and behaviour of one individual' (*Ballad* 83). From this interpretative belief comes Spark's preoccupation with the idea of lies and fiction in her novels. Beginning with her first novel, *The Comforters* (1957), she has explored in all her work the role of the novelist and the writing of fiction. This urge to expose the illusion that fiction is reality is what makes her novels metafictional, obsessively returning to the relationship between fiction and reality. Dougal, the troubling protagonist of the *Ballad*, is presented throughout as a supreme manipulator of reality and illusion, until he finally manifests as a novelist in the last chapter:

Thereafter, for economy's sake, he gathered together the scrap ends of his profligate experience – for he was a frugal man at heart – and turned them into a lot of cockeyed books, and went far in the world (142).

Dougal's fate in the novel is to be a survivor and representative of the novelist as liar, frugally presenting his 'cockeyed' works to the world. The novel is a presentation of Dougal's disturbing movement as an unsettling force through the working and lower middle class milieu of Peckham Rye, crooked, reliable only in his unreliability, rewriting the scripts for the lives of the other characters while ghosting the autobiography of Maria Cheeseman creatively out of their stories:

> 'I thought it was a work of art you wanted to write,' Dougal said, 'now was that not so? If you only want to write a straight autobiography you should have got a straight ghost. I'm crooked' (76).

Spark has said that she always starts with a title and then works around different meanings: 'a novel is, for me, always an elaboration of a title'(Kemp, 72)[2]. *The Ballad of Peckham Rye* is an expression of those ballads that were ingrained in her in childhood. The novel contains the characteristics we expect in the ballads: a tale told objectively and impersonally in a detached manner, often through dialogue, with repetition, sudden shifts in time, and the juxtaposition of the supernatural and the everyday, sudden death, all told in simple language, using formulaic phrases and repetitions, and with very little extended description. Spark uses the same techniques as the ballads in all her fiction but what she also does in the *Ballad* is to play with the idea of the oral tradition where material is handed down, altered, half-remembered, or improved to fit the occasion. Chapter One, in particular, is presented in a kind of flowing orality, reworking the material of one event which takes place well towards the end of chronological time in the narrative, Humphrey's return to Peckham and Dixie's house after having stood her up at the altar a few weeks' before. The first words of the novel, 'Get away from here, you dirty swine' are by Dixie's mother, Mavis. 'She slammed the door in his face' (7). She reports this event to her family, adjusting the dialogue to make her seem more decisive and infusing it with the repetitive rhythms of 'he said' 'I said'; in her opening conversation it had been her actions that were more decisive than her words:

> 'He said, "Hallo, Mavis," he said. I said, "You just hop it, you." He said, "Can I see Dixie?" I said, "You certainly can't," I said. I said,

"You're a dirty swine. You remove yourself," I said, "and don't show your face again," I said. He said, "Come on, Mavis." I said, "Mrs Crewe to you," and I shut the door in his face' (11).

The main concern of the first chapter is to move us back and forth between events and reported events, showing the oral tradition in practice with the movement of information and misinformation around a small urban community. The whole chapter revolves around Humphrey's desertion of Dixie at the altar. At the first pub Humphrey enters, the information floats in the air, coming from an invisible narrator in colloquial tones, 'he was that fellow that walked out on his wedding a few weeks ago' (7); in the second pub, a woman remarks 'It wouldn't have happened if Dougal Douglas hadn't come here' (7). This leads to a direct report of the wedding and the tension between Dixie and Humphrey over Dougal Douglas:

'I want to catch your cold. I like to think of the germs hopping from you to me.' 'I know where you got all these disgusting ideas from. You got them from Dougal Douglas. Well, I'm glad he's gone and there won't be him at the wedding to worry about in case he starts showing off the lumps on his head or something.' 'I liked Dougal,' Humphrey said (8).

Chapter One presents most of the characters of the novel within the construction of a folk tale. After the fight Humphrey has with Trevor Lomax outside the first pub:

various witnesses . . . were putting the story together . . . . Before closing time the story had spread to the surrounding public bars, where it was established that Humphrey had called at 12 Rye Grove earlier in the evening (12–13) . . . . But in any case, within a few weeks, everyone forgot the details. The affair is a legend referred to from time to time in the pubs when the conversation takes a matrimonial turn. Some say the bridegroom came back repentant and married the girl in the end. Some say, no, he married another girl, while the bride married the best man. It is wondered if the bride had been carrying on with the best man for some time past. It is sometimes told that the bride died of grief and the groom shot himself on the Rye. It is generally agreed that he answered 'No' at his wedding, that he went away alone on his wedding day and turned up again later (14).

All the speculations, symptomatic of the kind of rolling, discursive story telling of the oral tradition, are of the classic ballad scenarios of betrayal and unfaithful love. The story is 'put together' until the affair becomes 'a legend', reminding us of the beginning of the Editor's narrative in Hogg's *Confessions of a Justified Sinner*, which appeals to tradition 'for the remainder of the motley adventures of that house' (Hogg, 1); this appeal to oral tradition as an accurate source of information is the first hint by Hogg of the unreliability of the Editor's narrative. There is a litany of people in Chapter One who hear the news of Humphrey's return, concluding:

> lastly by mid-morning break at Meadows Meade the occurrence was known to all on the floor such as Dawn Waghorn, cone-winder, Annette Wren, trainee-seamer, Elaine Kent, process-controller, Odette Hill, up-twister, Raymond Lowther, packer, Lucille Potter, gummer; and it was revealed also to the checking department and many of the stackers, the sorters and the Office (13–14).

This invokes the specific reality of work at Meadows, Meade and Grindley, manufacturers of nylon textiles, establishing the verisimilitude of the factory. But it also provides the naming of Elaine Kent's role, 'process-controller', as the one person who is fully aware of Dougal's doubleness, understanding the process by which Dougal constructs and manipulates his roles as Dougal Douglas or Douglas Dougal, the names providing the mirror image of his own doubleness: 'What's your game, Dougal? . . . I better call you Doug, and be done with it' (70).

The earlier passage concludes with those who did not hear the news:

> Miss Merle Coverdale, lately head of the typing pool, did not hear of it. Mr Druce, lately Managing Director, did not hear of it. Neither did Dougal Douglas, the former Arts man, nor his landlady Miss Belle Frierne who had known all Peckham in her youth (14).

These last four are set aside by the concluding melancholy rhythms of 'lately', 'lately', 'did not hear', 'neither', 'nor'. '[A]ll Peckham' that will feature in the novel thus appears in Chapter One in person or by report. The looping circularity of Spark's customary pattern of non-linear narrative, with its proleptic simultaneity of past, present and future, detonating surprise, is echoed in the rhythms and repetitions of the reported speech. Spark in her book on John Masefield describes the border ballads as being 'concerned with the lyrical winding in and out of a situation; for all their repetitiveness and length, they are models of narrative economy . . . we get a compiled narrative – a sequence of events stated in such a way that they have the power to suggest what is left unsaid, the logical connections' (1953, 104). This presages her own fictional style, the 'lyrical winding in and out', 'the power to suggest what is left unsaid', in the spareness of the language and the repetitive construction of her tightly organised narrative structures. Spark finds in the border ballads what became her ineradicable trademarks, the ballads being in the bloodstream of the Spark novels, with her last but one novel, *Symposium* (1990), as interlinked as the *Ballad* to Scottish traditions, the same cross referencing to Hogg's *Confessions* in its central character Margaret, the same misdirection of attention culminating in sudden death from an unexpected direction.

Dougal Douglas's name is a running thread in Chapter One, someone who caused things to happen, who changed people and then left. He is protagonist and catalyst, a 'people-watcher and behaviourist', as Spark describes herself (*Curriculum Vitae* 25), who manipulates the reality around him and meta-morphoses himself through many forms, mirroring what his companions are or want to be, treating 'mimesis not as repetition but as sport, a one-off contest between himself and the forces of banality' (Craig, 1993, 77). He is the Gilmartin of Peckham Rye, and like Gilmartin in *Confessions*, there is an ambiguity about his reality: a devil or angel, a manipulative stranger, a projection of people's imaginations. He appears directly in Chapter Two when he is interviewed by Mr Druce for a post in personnel; a Cambridge time and motion man has already speeded up output by thirty percent: 'he worked out the simplest pattern of movement involving the least loss of en-ergy and time' (16), and absenteeism has become a problem in the factory. Dougal, 'in a split second of absent-mindedness' (17) speculates that they must be bored; it is only in that 'split-second' that Dougal permits reality through the normal screen of his play-acting. Otherwise he is continually presenting himself in a controlled and self–conscious variety of personae, as the author-manipulator, 'God' and devil, who metamorphoses shape con-stantly and induces transformations in his surroundings by his actions. In his second meeting with Druce he becomes in turn a judge, an analyst, a lady-columnist, and a prosecution counsel, 'grave, lean, and inquisitorial' (65–67). For Mr Willis, managing director of Drover Willis, the textile manufacturers of Peckham, Dougal becomes Douglas Dougal and changes his manner, 'for he perceived that Mr Willis was a Scot' (68); he becomes 'a solid steady Edinburgh boy, all the steadier for the hump on his shoulder' (69); and in the night club he transforms himself through a sequence with a dustbin lid, as a man in a rowing boat, a Zulu dancer, a Chinese coolie, an ardent cyclist, an old woman with an umbrella, a man in a canoe spearing fish, and ends up as the band-leader who 'limply conducted an invisible band' (59–60). At his first appearance in the novel,

> Dougal, who in the University Dramatics had taken the part of Rizzio in a play about Mary, Queen of Scots, leaned forward and put all his energy into his own appearance; he dwelt with a dark glow on Mr Druce, he raised his right shoulder, which was already highly crooked by nature, and leaned on his elbow with a becoming twist of the body. Dougal put Mr Druce through the process of his smile, which was wide and full of white young teeth; he made movements with the alarming bones of his hands. Mr Druce could not keep his eyes off Dougal, as Dougal perceived (15).

Douglas's shoulder, 'highly crooked by nature', exemplifies his movement through the everyday world of Peckham, insinuating himself always into unexpected angles and positions. By naming Rizzio as Dougal's University part, Spark couples him with the compelling Italian musician, favoured by Mary and killed in front of her in 1566 at Holyrood House by supporters of her husband jealous of Rizzio's advancement and influence. Rizzio's name transforms Dougal into the exotic outsider to the community, the Scots graduate in the socially precarious upper working / lower middle class milieu of Peckham Rye. He looks out on the class borders from his lodging, 'the back gardens belonging to the opposite street of houses . . . neglected, overgrown and packed with junk and sheds for motor-bicycles, not neat like Miss Frierne's [Dougal's landlady] and the row of gardens on the near side, with their borders and sometimes a trellis bower' (21–22), people-watching as he assesses the 'classes within classes in Peckham' (29), reflecting back the constrictions and banality of their lives to the inhabitants of Peckham. But Spark's reference to Rizzio is also hinting at danger, jealousy and death, carrying resonances of the betrayal, murder and death that are the staple fare of ballads. That becomes the fate of Mr Druce, fascinated into sexual yearning for Dougal, trapped in an automatic affair with Merle, the head of the typing pool, taking off their clothes 'in a steady rhythm' (53), punctuated by Druce's sadistic pinches and bites. Druce toys with a paper-knife and a corkscrew in Merle's presence, Dougal talks of her long neck as 'a maniac's delight' (82, 136, 101), presaging her sudden murder by Mr Druce: 'He came towards her with the corkscrew and stabbed it into her long neck nine times, and killed her. Then he took his hat and went home to his wife' (136). The 'living a lie' of Druce's marriage, Dougal's 'fatal flaw' of fear of illness, the red wine that Merle drinks (the 'blude red wine' of the ballads), the 'nine times' of Merle's stabbing, are all the formulaic repetitions of the ballads with which Spark signals the tale of jealousy and murder that constitutes the ballad of Merle's death, hinted at from the first mention of her name, 'poor Miss Coverdale' (12), and finally enacted casually by Druce. Rizzio, the dark, long dead foreigner play-acted in another country, represents an uneasy hint of the danger surrounding Dougal.

Dougal's Scottishness is foregrounded: 'the Scotch man' (13), who had been thought frivolous in the Edinburgh pubs, 'not being a Nationalist' (22), and who claims feyness from his Highland blood (67). He is a Scot, like Richard Willis of Drover Willis, Dougal's second employer, who is seen as outside the English class system (119). The people of Peckham Rye comment on his strangeness, his difference. One periphery is the same as another to them: 'Thought he was Irish from his voice . . . . Irish sounds a bit like Scotch like, to hear it' (19). Half-Irish Elaine specifically connects the two: 'One thing about you I'll admit . . . you're different. If I didn't know you were Scotch I'd swear you were Irish. My mother's Irish' (63). It is Dougal's difference and separateness which allows him to move fluidly through the subtly different class positions, performing transitions not open to the residents of Peckham Rye. And Dougal brings the disruption and disturbing force of the outsider to this world. He mirrors this outsider role in his dream, Spark foregrounding and having Dougal acknowledge his similarity to the infinitely changeable devil:

> 'I have a dream at nights,' Dougal said ' . . . of girls in factories do-ing a dance with only the movements of their breasts, bottoms, and arms as they sort, stack, pack, check, cone-wind, gum, uptwist, as-semble, seam, and set. I see the Devil in the guise of a chap from Cambridge who does motion-study, and he's the choreographer . . . . And . . . of course this choreographer is a projection of me. I was at the University of Edinburgh myself, but in the dream I'm the Devil and Cambridge' (50).

Like Gilmartin and Mr Wringhim who speak in English in *Confessions*, in his dream Dougal mischievously changes himself from Scotsman into the English class outsider from Cambridge who had imposed time and motion methods onto the workers. Dougal's outsider status ensures a mystery at the heart of his separateness; his duality is between this world and another: either he is a mischievous, self-important manipulator of other people, editor of their stories, a coward afraid of illness, 'sickness kills me' (24), who

leaves Peckham when he finds his landlady dying of a stroke; or he is a
spirit ruining souls, a devil creating mayhem and death, while claiming to
transform the daily dreariness of the lives of workers in Peckham Rye; or
he is both simultaneously. Spark insists on the simultaneity of different
possibilities: Dougal showing off his bumps as incipient devil's horns, yet
denying to Humphrey that he was the Devil, 'I'm only supposed to be one
of the wicked spirits that wander through the world for the ruin of souls'
(77); and Dougal telling Merle:

> 'I have powers of exorcism . . . that's all.' 'What's that?' 'The ability
> to drive devils out of people.' 'I thought you said you were a devil
> yourself.' 'The two states are not incompatible' (102).

Spark emphasises Dougal's inconsistency and ambiguity; he's an angel-devil,
he's destructive, but he brings the virtues of clarity, openness and excitement as well as danger to Peckham's inhabitants, bringing 'lyricism to the
concept' (26) of language and life, organising appearance and reality in
his surroundings, allowing Spark to extend her metafictional exploration,
denying us the illusion that fiction is reality.

Spark opposes Dougal with Nelly Mahone, the homeless woman, whose
role is 'to go out on her rounds proclaiming' (80), her biblical quotations
providing an oblique commentary, reporting to Dougal and those who have
ears to hear what is happening, providing the reader with an interpretative
moral counterpoint and commentary on Dougal's character. '[A]t her post',
on her first appearance, she comments 'for all to hear, "Praise be to God
who employs the weak to confound the strong and whose ancient miracles
we see shining even in our time" '(13). In the circular pattern of the novel,
Nellie's commentary in Chapter One comes chronologically after Dougal
has left Peckham, and has to be reread in its position in the first chapter
to produce the intentional resonances of the weak confounding the strong,
the people of Peckham confounding the force of darkness, Dougal. His ally
until he offends her, 'I don't know whether I'm coming or going with you'
(114), Nelly's arrangements to meet Dougal to pass on information are
embedded in biblical phrases which carry a moral warning and a description
of Dougal's behaviour:

> Haughty eyes, a lying tongue, hands that shed innocent blood. See
> me in the morning. A heart that deviseth wicked plots, feet that are
> swift to run into mischief. Ten at Paley's yard. A deceitful witness
> that uttereth lies. Meeting-house Lane. And him that soweth discord
> among brethren (107).

This passage occurs as Dougal, Humphrey, Elaine and Dixie go into the pub where Trevor, maddened by Dougal's mockery of him ('He's got you, Trev. He does Trevor to a T' [110]), breaks his glass and, lunging past Dougal who takes avoiding action, pushes it full into Humphrey's face, shedding the blood of the innocent. But Merle's innocent blood is also to be shed, by the Dougal-obsessed Druce. Nelly's final meeting with Dougal contains her moral judgement on him, declaimed to the air outside the pub:

'The words of the double-tongued are as if they were harmless, but they reach even to the inner part of the bowels. Praise be to the Lord, who distinguishes our cause and delivers us from the unjust and deceitful man.' ... As they passed, Nelly spat on the pavement (132).

Dougal is 'the double-tongued' who speaks ambiguously. Trevor insists that the random phrases in Dougal's stolen notebook are 'a code .... Autumn means something else. Everything means something' (92), which reminds us to read everything with double eyes, as Sandy and Jenny had listened with 'double ears'(*Prime*, 18) to Jean Brodie. The archaeological excavations into the layered past lives of Peckham with the subterranean messages from the past being gradually exposed, provide a metaphor for the layered meanings within the novel. They are also a means for Dougal's escape from Peckham under the Rye, appropriate for his ambiguous status as one who fears to cross the water (like Burns's witches in 'Tam o' Shanter') but who is at home in that underground passage suggestive of the borderlines between this world and the next. In Spark's fictional world, the natural and super-natural coexist easily; 'as you might say there was another world than this' (143) are the closing words of the novel. As in the world of folk traditions, spirits can move between worlds, and miraculous occurrences are possible. Unease may be the result, but certainty and ambiguity coexist. 'The two states are not incompatible'(102) is applicable to spiritual presence in the daily life of any of Spark's created worlds, including Peckham Rye. Nelly's 'ancient miracles we see shining even in our times' (13) transform their lives so that the Rye, flowing through the novel and Peckham, looks at the end to Humphrey, 'for an instant ... like a cloud of green and gold, the people seeming to ride upon it', suggesting that 'there was another world than this' (143). Like Hogg, Spark assumes alternative interpretations, writing certainty and unease into the structure of her novels.

Notes

1. Calvinism and Muriel Spark's works, including the *Ballad*, are explored in Glenda Norquay, *Moral Absolutism in the Novels of Robert Louis Stevenson, Robin Jenkins and Muriel Spark: Challenges to Realism. Unpublished Ph.D thesis.* Edinburgh: University of Edinburgh, 1985. See also Allan Massie, *Muriel Spark*, chap.1. Massie thinks the *Ballad* 'a relative failure' (30).
2. This interview is untraced; Kemp mistakenly cites *The Scotsman* 20 Aug. 1962 as the source.

Works Cited

Craig, Cairns 'Doubtful Imaginings The Sceptical Art of Muriel Spark', *Études Écossaises*. vol. 2 G.D.R. *Études Écossaises*: Grenoble, 1993, 63–77
Hogg, James *The Private Memoirs and Confessions of a Justified Sinner.* 1824; Oxford: OUP, 1970
Kemp, Peter *Muriel Spark*. London: Elek, 1974
Massie, Allan *Muriel Spark*. Edinburgh: Ramsay Head, 1979
Spark, Muriel *The Ballad of Peckham Rye*. 1960; Harmondsworth: Penguin, 1963
Spark *Curriculum Vitae*. London: Constable, 1992
Spark *John Masefield*. London: Peter Nevill, 1953
Spark *The Prime of Miss Jean Brodie*. 1961; Harmondsworth: Penguin, 1965
Spark *Symposium*. 1990; Harmondsworth: Penguin, 1991

Spark, Muriel: articles and interviews

Ex-S. BBC TV Scotland, 29 Jan.1996
Jenkins, Alan *Sunday Times*. 13 March 1988
Kermode, Frank 'The House of Fiction', *Partisan Review*. vol.30. spring 1963; rpbd. in Malcolm Bradbury ed. *Novel Today*. Manchester: Fontana and Manchester University Press, 1977, 131–35
Spark 'How I Became a Novelist', *John O'London's*. vol.3. 1 Dec.1960, 683
Spark 'My Conversion', *Twentieth Century*. vol. 170. Autumn 1961, 58–63

A Far Cry from the Kailyard: Jessie Kesson's *Glitter of Mica*

Isobel Murray

Jessie Kesson determinedly resisted adjectives like feminist and feminine. From her position, education and experience, feminine meant passive, soft, weak. She wrote to Letizia Accinelli in 1987: 'My principal female characters . . . were themselves of a more than usual anti-feminine mind. They were individual and strongminded' (Accinelli,1990, 4). But just as clearly modern feminism will see her characters as quintessentially female, and will recognise her work as constituting trenchant expression of the position of oppressed or potentially oppressed women in a patriarchal Scottish society. I have argued elsewhere:

> [b]ut she never saw gender issues as isolated, separated from the complex of social and economic issues that imprisoned farm workers in tiny worlds, and in tied houses from which they could be evicted at the farmer's whim every six months. So feminist issues or gender issues certainly concern her, but perhaps never exclusively so (Hewitt,1995,182).

In *Glitter of Mica*, which she frequently said was her own favourite novel, she made a unique attempt to face all these issues together, to outline the human predicament as it presents itself in twentieth-century Scotland. Although the book is strong in humour and fortitude, it presents a bleak picture of human life, recalling the pessimistic view of Grassic Gibbon's Diffusionism, that human kind went wrong when it accepted civilization, agriculture, institutions, and that now it is unbelievably difficult to become Hugh Riddel's ideal, a 'bonnie whole man' (109).

Here then Kesson's unique analysis of the half-life allowed to women is married to her analysis of a whole agricultural parish of Scotland – or of the world in little. Women are still shown to suffer most and to be acknowledged least, but the human condition is illustrated through the inhabitants of the parish, and in particular the male condition is rendered with a steady gaze through the character of Hugh Riddel, denied education yet aspirant, unable to understand his angry opposition to conventional civilization in the form of Charlie Anson, or his thwarted sexuality in his marriage to Isa, or to articulate fully his discontent with civilization as he finds it. It is also reinforced by Hugh's memories of his father's frustrations, which foreshadow his own experience of marital frigidity without helping him to avoid it.

In *The White Bird Passes, Where the Apple Ripens* and *Another Time, Another Place*, Kesson tended to construct her fiction out of her own life experience – and arguably constructed her own life for herself by doing so, forging an identity, becoming her own creator where no other was evident (Hewitt, 1995). But *Glitter of Mica* was her favourite because it is a very different work. It attempts the same kind of breadth of vision as male authors had always assumed to be their right, portraying both sexes with insight and compassion. The canvas is thus much wider, and she simultaneously chronicles and criticises a whole agricultural parish, its class rigidities, its social inequalities, its grim and joyless marriages and coarse and cruel sexual attitudes. By retracing Hugh Riddel's memories of childhood, the novel also acquires a dimension of history, recounting the barbaric conditions of farm workers before the Second World War, and tracing the failed relationship of Hugh Riddel's parents as well as the catastrophic privacies of his own marriage.

So *Glitter of Mica* is a very ambitious novel, where Kesson uniquely chooses a male protagonist, and involves a large cast of characters and three generations of Riddels. But its peculiar impact is the result of its complex structure and narrative method. In it, Kesson telescopes and compresses all this material onto the events of a single night. Where the other novels relate their events with rare economy, precision and clarity, the structure of *Glitter of Mica* is such that it is hard even to follow the narrative at first reading. We are wooed into reading not for the intensely dramatic events of the story line, but for the struggles of different characters to understand themselves, their lives, their sexual needs or what is happening around them. It is a truly democratic, twentieth-century tragedy. It is not divided into chapters, only punctuated at intervals by a row of asterisks, so there are thirty-three unnumbered sections. This lulls the reader into acceptance of a very unorthodox presentation.

The first of these sections makes no attempt to single out individual characters, but introduces the unprepossessing parish of Aberdeenshire appropriately known as Caldwell. The description of this parish 'to the east of our shire' is primarily negative: '[i]t has moved neither poet to song nor tourist to praise. It has little to give or lend but much to sell' (7). Its landmarks are the Pictish Horse on Soutar Hill, the old Free Kirk which is now, significantly, a granary, and Ambroggan House, a hospital for 'the wealthy mentally ill of the land' (11). The parish is surrounded by old houses and castles occupied by old names, but these are diminished by the fact that the first we see is the absurd Lady Grizelda Beaton opening last summer's Show, 'prancing and gesticulating' to the scorn of the farm-workers who will be central to the book, providing a down-to-earth commentary: we are told here that 'Caldwell is first and foremost the land of the farm-worker' (9). The wry comments and often cruel laughter of the farm-workers punctuate the novel, repeatedly deflating, gossiping and parochially jeering.

The author meantime takes particular care not to apprise the reader of the dramatic facts of the story. After the introductory section, we move into some thirty pages of Hugh Riddel's youthful memories. The first-time reader has no way of knowing that Hugh Riddel is currently waiting to hear whether his daughter Helen will survive a road accident – or suicide attempt? – the previous Friday, after her father attacked her seducer, his longterm rival Charlie Anson. The re-reader is likely to wonder at the detachment of these memories: apart from trying to avert his eyes from Ambroggan House, where Helen lies between life and death, Hugh gives no great sign of distress, or anxiety about his daughter, but reflects instead on his own youth, his father's repeated experience of cottardom, tied houses and 'the sack without words' (13), his parents' marriage, his own youthful happiness, his disillusionment by his own unhappy, sexually frustrated marriage, and the immediate ordeal of going into the Dairy and facing his fellow workers. Is Hugh in denial, or does he not care about his daughter at all?

The narrator now apparently settles down to describe the events of last Friday night, but it is a long time before we hear any more of the drama, which is not the central purpose of the book. We are now to see virtually the whole parish preparing for their usual Friday night, and to inhabit the points of view of several characters before the drama briefly recurs: clearly, plot is not the main concern here. We see the ladies stepping Kirkwards and the farm-workers' wives going to the Women's Rural – and we hear what both the ladies ('guardians') and the farm-workers' wives ('critics') have to say about Hugh Riddel's 'Immortal Memory' speech the previous week. The text here amounts to a multiply focused account of Riddel's speech, and as the novel progresses we find longer passages presenting and analysing Sue Tatt and her family, the down-trodden Isa Riddel and the humiliated Helen Riddel. These seem almost purposely drained of their drama.

The novel that results from this method succeeds in illuminating not one major character but at least four, and the general experience of their lives, not just these two nights, with a pungent group of farm-workers functioning as chorus. It allows the presentation of the parish, a small society riven by class prejudice, precedence and notions of respectability, where the characters are trapped in demanding toil and unrewarding lives, many deprived of dignity by the very nature of the cottar life, and deprived of sexual fulfilment by the repressive mores that live on, although we are told at the start that 'the people of Caldwell are less kirk conscious than were their forebears' (7). (We soon learn, however, that the genteel middle classes have a different view).

In his sensitive Introduction to the 1982 reprint of the novel, William Donaldson points out that 'none of the characters are complete people (5)'. Helen Riddel ponders the idea of 'the "bonnie whole man" her father was always on about. But was there anyone at all bonnie and whole? Was anyone at all completely so?' (109). She concludes that someone *might* grow up so, 'if one was not begotten, but fell out of the sky, a second old, to land on Soutar Hill maybe.' No parents, no oppressive nurture, no company, no language, and no deceiving words. A bleak vision – but Caldwell is described as bleak four times in the first few pages. By having both Hugh and Helen Riddel question the wholeness of modern human kind, and by presenting such an analysis of the lack of wholeness, Kesson seems to move for once from concentration on the social oppression of individual women by the pressures of a class-ridden and primitive patriarchal society, often enforced by well-trained women, to a resistance to human society generally, almost an echo of some of the anti-civilization passages of *A Scots Quair*. The title of *Glitter of Mica* comes of course from G. S. Fraser's poem 'Home Town Elegy', but that does not preclude *Glitter of Mica* challenging a memory of *Grey Granite*.

Kesson confronts Scottish literary traditions in *Glitter of Mica* with a brisk dismissal of sentimental Kailyard values. She tackles the soothing literary myths of Scotland as determinedly as Hugh MacDiarmid in *A Drunk Man*, if less explicitly. While she uses the life of Robert Burns to expose the destructive nature of small town society from Mauchline to Caldwell, she takes fundamental issue, as experienced cottar herself, with the sentimental effusions of Burns' 'The Cotter's Saturday Night'. References to Burns' life and more respectful references to other poems permeate the novel, but

everything comes back to that poem. *Glitter of Mica*, we might say, deliberately concerns itself with two contrasting and sequential instances of 'The
Cottar's Friday Night', one on which Hugh Riddel is (rather surprisingly)
asked to propose the Immortal Memory, and the next, on which he mur-
derously attacks his longterm rival, also his daughter's seducer. There are
ironic echoes of Burns here too:

> Is there in human-form, that wears a heart
> – A wretch! a villain! lost to love and truth!
> That can, with studied, sly, ensnaring art,
> Betray sweet Jenny's unsuspecting youth? (stanza 10)

The attack on Burns' idealised picture of the farm-worker's life and sexual
mores is direct and effective.

In an interview in 1985, Kesson was full of a new insight into her work.
She quoted a line from *The White Bird Passes*, 'Queer folk who were oot
and who, perversely enough, never had any desire to be in'(*The White Bird
Passes*, 1958,118; 1996,112; see also Murray, 1996, 58). She went on to
survey her work:

> Every work I've ever written contains ae 'ootlin'. Lovely Aberdeenshire
> word. Somebody that never really fitted into the thing . . . It's always
> aboot people who don't fit in! Now, I know mysel at last and it's just
> in one line in that book where fowk were oot who never had ony
> desire to be in (Murray, 1996, 58).

Glitter of Mica takes this helpful insight further. The wider focus makes a
more general statement here. Janie in *The White Bird Passes* learned to value
privacy and dignity as defences against the world, as did Isabel Emslie in
Where the Apple Ripens, and the young woman in *Another Time, Another
Place*: public disgrace and humiliation were the ultimate in suffering. But
in *Glitter of Mica* we have a whole cast of stunted, thwarted, incomplete
characters, many of whom have to learn, like Helen Riddel, to settle for a
Charlie Anson instead of the impossible 'bonnie whole man', or like Hugh
Riddel's father, to settle for an abject, oppressed way of life in a tied cottage,
where sacking without words could be a six-monthly occurrence. All these
major characters can be seen as 'ootlins': indeed, in this society there is no
community, and no real possibility of relationships, or belonging. The effect
of Kesson's bizarre structure is that we can examine each in turn, and experience the narrator's understanding and compassion for all the unhappy
characters, save Anson.

Hugh Riddel is unusual, an exceptional farm-worker. Denied any coher-
ent education, he has risen on merit, and is much thought of by his farmer
Darklands and others on the Rural Council. He raised hackles when he accepted the invitation to propose the Immortal Memory at a Burns supper.
Hugh admires and in some ways idealises Burns, but unlike his mistress
Sue Tatt, who succumbs to the lure of Kailyard fiction when she names her
daughter Fiona, after a romantic heroine, 'her eyes always set wide apart
and grey' (68), Hugh is immune to sentimental bardolatry. He privately
hates what he thinks of as the 'smarm' of 'The Cotter's Saturday Night':
'The lines grued in Hugh Riddel's mind. It was easily seen that such a poem
was written by a man who ploughed his *own* furrows. Never by a fee'd
ploughman' (34–5). Here he separately comes to share some of Helen's pes-
simism about the possibility of wholeness: 'It was just that no man could
come into good estate free of that which and those who had preceded him'
(35).

In his public speech Riddel had upset the Misses Lennox, by describing
the harsh realities of Burns' life compared to those in Caldwell: we catch his
gist and their indignation simultaneously in Kesson's economical narration.
Taking a leaf out of MacDiarmid's book, he had told them that half of
them 'would have no more meed for Burns himself if he were to settle down
amongst them tomorrow, than the "unco guid" had for him in Mauchline
in his own day' (53). (Compare *A Drunk Man*, ll.43–4, 'And gin there was
his like alive the day / They'd be the last a kennin' haund to gie'). He had
pursued this analogy of Mauchline and Caldwell, pointing out that in small
town Scotland 'Burns would have been left with little choice but to marry
Jean Armour' (53): the disgrace would be too great. And divorce was as
unlikely in either place.

Hugh Riddel revealingly sees Burns as a striving but fated idealist:

he had needed the impossible. To have one foot on the front step of
the castle, and the other trailing behind on the dunghill, and never
both together, was just about the loneliest thing that could ever befall
a man, and the woman wasn't born who could have bridged this gap
with Burns. But . . . that had never prevented Burns from searching
for her, and even glimpsing her fleeting reflection in the faces of all
women (54).

Again, MacDiarmid's *Drunk Man* has suggested something of what this
other Hugh is trying to articulate: in the section sometimes known as 'The
Feminine Principle' (ll.933–976), he compares himself with Burns on the

matter of women, and considers the end of marriage not necessarily being to produce children:

> ... a sairer task
> Is aiblins to create oorsels
> As we can be – it's that I ask.

And this section ends with an aspiration not unlike Hugh Riddel's:

> He's no' a man ava',
> And lacks a proper pride,
> Gin less than a' the warld
> Can ser' him for a bride! ...

Is this the ideal of the 'bonnie whole man'? The Misses Lennox are offended by Riddel's version of the sentiments of *A Drunk Man*, 'As Kirks wi' Christianity ha'e dune, / Burns Clubs wi' Burns' (ll.109–10). They are reminded of the miner turned lay preacher who had accused his congregation of 'being quite capable of crucifying Christ again because they lacked recognition':

> A recollection which rankled particularly with the Misses Lennox, for it was one of their great dreams and small hopes that, for His Second Coming, Christ would choose Caldwell, convinced that they would be the first to recognise Him, after a lifetime acquaintance with Holman Hunt's *Light of the World* in their front parlour (56).

In contrast to the genteel ladies, the farm-workers' wives are part proud, part envious of Hugh Riddel. They descend quickly to personalities, voicing general dislike for Charlie Anson (at whom, they say, Riddel stared throughout his rendition of 'Holy Willie's Prayer'), and in part at least acknowledging the truth of Hugh Riddel's analysis to their own experience.

Sue Tatt is one of Kesson's most interesting fictional creations. She is a mature woman with teenage children, and she has largely evaded the stifling conventions of the town by determinedly remaining an ootlin, an outsider who acknowledges the sex drive, believes in kindness, and had her glory days in the relaxed atmosphere of war time on the Home Front. Caldwell thinks of her as disreputable and 'easy', but then, 'Caldwell was seldom charitable towards its own' (63). Sue knows herself better than most characters do, and is conscious of conflicting roles competing for her performance, 'a widow woman, bringing up a young family, all on her own', 'just an ordinary housewife', 'a woman of the world', Helen of Troy, and even potentially 'one of the most house-proud women in all Caldwell' (62–76). With all of this, Sue has retained more spontaneity than anyone else in the book, more zest for life, more emotional range.

She is insecure about her reception by farm-workers' wives (which varies according to whether she meets them alone, or in pairs or more), and about her physical attractiveness, where she craves her daughter's tributes. Fiona, the narrator tells us, understands her mother, and their relationship is close, if stormy: 'Fiona was the only one of her children that Sue Tatt really liked; and then simply as one human being likes another' (67). We remember Hugh's father telling him of the very minimal essentials for marriage, at least lust or liking. Sue resents Fiona's understanding: 'No two people should ever have such an intimate uncomfortable knowing of each other' (131). But the narrator takes leave to qualify this, making Sue seem the nearest we can find in the novel to 'bonnie and whole':

> Half her life, Sue thought resentfully when Fiona had gone, was spent in taking it out of her daughter, and the other half in atoning for that.
>   Had you at any other time tried to explain to Sue Tatt that, far from dividing her life, this relationship was one which gave it wholeness, she would have rejected you. But not now, not at this particular moment, when she was dimly perceiving that for herself (131).

When it comes to rendering Isa Riddel, Kesson shows remarkable understanding and compassion. Her own favourite female characters may have been 'individual and strongminded', but she knew exactly how women were manoeuvred into Isa's subservient, frightened and hopeless situation. Again, Isa is in many ways a replica of Hugh Riddel's own mother. He watched his mother 'diminish' his father and resist his sexuality, even heard her say, '[t]he trouble with you is you should have married some great roaring quean who was more your like' (42). But he married a woman 'not unlike' his mother (39), and suffered deeply from his wife's frigidity. The difference is that Hugh perceives 'a good wife could bind you prisoner forever . . . God! but I had to burst myself out and free, Hugh Riddel thought' (31). He found Sue Tatt, and both pitied and envied his father for not doing likewise.

When we finally get glimpses of Isa, we do not expect to pity her too much: we have heard too much of Hugh's disgust, as in his ambition to murder her in an imaginary speech to Helen (40). But she turns out to be more sympathetic. She is very conscious of being an ootlin, of 'a feeling of outwithness' (82), but she does not give up hope: she blurts out words to

the amused children on the Scholars' train, and to the Commercial Travel-
ler she meets there – 'she hadn't spoken so freely to anyone in years' (85).
She silently faces her disappointment over Helen – Isa's prestige had risen
sharply when Helen, a lass o' pairts, went to university; but to her uncom-
prehending and brainwashed mother, Helen's taking a Diploma in Social
Science had 'just seemed a come-down from an M.A.' (87).
   She is afraid of Hugh, and always anticipates his strangling impatience.
The same Friday night, she 'gabbles' her news to Hugh, 'knowing that anything she said would be wrong, but always hoping to find something that
would be right' (122). He is angry, pitiless, bullying. She sees their mutual
isolation, and tries to recapture her sense of her younger self, Isa Mavor.
But this only happens accidentally on occasion, as when she picks wild
flowers like the young woman in *Another Time, Another Place*: ' . . . had
she found a mirror then, Isa Riddel might for an instant have looked on Isa
Mavor' (123). Now she has again tempted Hugh to murder: the relationship
is hopeless, but both are helpless.
   When Helen hovers between life and death, it is Isa, not Hugh, who
seems truly affected, and Darklands' offer of a job-shift is for her sake.
But the final confrontation is doomed to noncommunication, one crucial
theme of the novel. Hugh believes 'nothing . . . ever came out of herself,
except her protestations, and these were but contradictions of his own
opinions' (150). But grief over Helen lends her 'voice for everything except itself' (151). The conflict is described in terms of a hostile sex attack:
'the preliminaries . . . that moment of giving and receiving – that instant of
fusion' (152). He sees the kindness of neighbours as mere curiosity, while
Isa defends some basic human values in the people of Caldwell, which we
must want to believe may be there. For once she becomes eloquent here,
but of course Hugh is not listening.
   Did Hugh Riddel love his daughter? Did she love him, and did she commit
suicide because of his virtual rejection? These are questions the text does
not enable us to answer with certainty. Are there *any* instances in the novel,
apart perhaps from Sue Tatt and her daughter, where any conventional instance of human love is to be found? Helen has the doubtful privilege of her
education, which has cut her off from her father, her community and her
native tongue, and equipped her with an illusory facility with words which
she easily sees through in the practice of her co-workers. She has sexual needs
as clamant as her father's, but no means of expressing them, as he does by
his very physical appearance, and she has no means of fully understanding
them until her sexual awakening at the hands of Charlie Anson. This is a
deep humiliation for her, that he discovers her needs at the same moment

as she does. She accepts the difference between Anson and her father's ideal of the 'bonnie whole man', and settles for Charlie, *faute de mieux*.

The fallibility of words and the failure of communication are central to the novel, and remarkably parallel to the failure, or at best partial success, of sexual relationships. Hugh cannot listen to Isa, and can only imagine telling Helen at cruel length why he wants to murder his wife. He and Sue Tatt have few words for each other. His attraction to Burns is partly at least to the articulacy which has been denied him, by family, school and society. But Hugh's own ability to use words, like his expression of his sexuality, is far above average. Both wife and daughter envy him. Isa could neither comprehend nor express her disappointed reaction to Helen's career in social work: 'It was Helen's father who had given words to it all . . . Hugh Riddel always did have the release of words' (87). Again the image is unsurprisingly sexual. Helen envies him because his sexuality is clearly expressed in his physical being, while she has never been able to express her own:

> It was easier for her father and his like. For all the male in him got out, gleamed in his leggings and glinted on the hairs of his hands . . . It was inside of him and it was outside of him.
>   But it was only inside herself (109).

Hugh's own response to Helen's education is an impatience with her use of words as labels:

> As though the correct word for them could cure them. Words like Delinquency, Hereditary, Environment, Behaviour Patterns. Whiles he felt like boring through that wall of words with which Helen had surrounded both herself and her vocation . . . (39–40).

It is at this point that he makes his imaginary speech to Helen, describing how he could kill Isa for the wrinkles in her stockings.

Helen's education had progressively affected her attitudes to words themselves. When she first went to university she learned English and became ashamed of Doric, and nagged her mother to follow suit. But a certain disenchantment with the world of social work her education opened out for her has taught her a new fondness for the old words: '[t]hey had become more than balm to her hearing now; they could sound her soul so that it leapt to the recognition of meaning again' (94).

A telling scene at the centre where she works underlines Helen's dissatisfaction with glib and easy language: Miss Booth sounds right, but becomes hollow with repetition, and Mr Fleming has just started a new 'buzz word' which everyone will adopt and overuse for a time (93). The wicked accuracy of observation reminds us that Kesson had long experience of social work, as well as cottaring. Helen and Charlie Anson are the characters who most clearly see through the power structures implicit in many uses of language. Both are aware that she can give him 'the words he was searching for . . . A lifetime of foolproof phrases', and that Helen is willing to be thus exploited as the price of sex, marriage and motherhood (136–7).

At the end of the novel, words fail as signifiers, but are necessary as ritual. We are never told for sure whether Helen meant to kill herself, but 'God Knows' and Hugh have to exchange certain phrases, on the one hand time-hallowed and on the other out-dated by loss of faith, 'the kind of words which had to be uttered by the one and heard by the other. You accepted death, but found the reason for it before burying the body' (155).

Works Cited

Accinelli, Maria Letizia, 'The Role of Women in Jessie Kesson's Fiction and Kesson's Treatment of Female Characters'. Unpublished M.Litt. thesis. Aberdeen: University of Aberdeen, 1990

Burns, Robert *Burns: Poems and Songs*. James Kingsley ed. Oxford: Oxford University Press, 1969

Donaldson, William 'Introduction' to *Glitter of Mica*. Edinburgh: Paul Harris, 1982, 1–6

Kesson, Jessie *Glitter of Mica*. London: Chatto and Windus, 1963; Edinburgh: Paul Harris,1982; London: Virago,1993 (identical pagination in each case)

Kesson, Jessie *The White Bird Passes*. London: Chatto and Windus, 1958; Edinburgh: B & W, 1996

MacDiarmid, Hugh, *A Drunk Man Looks at the Thistle*. Kenneth Buthlay ed. Edinburgh: Scottish Academic Press, 1987

Murray, Isobel 'Jessie Kesson; Writing Her Self', in *Northern Visions: Essays on the Literary Identity of Northern Scotland in the Twentieth Century*. David Hewitt ed. East Linton: Tuckwell Press, 1995, 180–189

Murray, Isobel ed., *Scottish Writers Talking: George Mackay Brown, Jessie Kesson, Norman MacCaig, William McIlvanney, David Toulmin Interviewed by Isobel Murray and Bob Tait*. East Linton: Tuckwell Press, 1996

A Select Bibliography of Scottish Women's Writing, 1920s to 1960s

Jennie Rubio

This bibliography provides a selective list of some writers and their works not discussed in the main body of this volume. New bibliographical, anthologising and republishing work, such as that by Catherine Kerrigan, Moira Burgess, Roderick Watson and others has made much material known and accessible to readers. What follows is merely intended to draw attention to some Scottish women writers not always considered.

Though many of these authors may seem unconcerned with nationalism, modernism, or even feminism, they are still of interest and they have made their own contribution to the development of twentieth century Scottish writing. They have, perhaps, been overlooked because of the way that the Scottish Renaissance has so often been defined, with the 'central' writers usually being seen as male. Much Scottish women's writing of this period has been criticised or ignored because it appeared to display 'Scottishness' in the wrong way – seemingly tainted with sentimentality, when the prevailing critical tendency has been the debunking of nostalgic myths of Scotland. This kind of writing was felt to be backward-looking, superseded by the work of modernists. Robert Elliot, for example, claimed that Glaswegian women writers had 'retreated into a shell of personal relationships, leaving to their male contemporaries not only the grimmer side of the city, but the major themes of industrial life. While the latter have given us the slums, the shipyards, politics, . . . the women novelists have tiptoed around the edge: a new dress, a wedding, a pining heart, but little more' (1982, 1). While Elliot's attitude now seems rather dated, the lack of consistent attention to the different varieties of writing by women echoes his assumption that much women's writing, typified by O. Douglas' series of novels about manse life, 'evok[es] an atmosphere of faded curtains and prayer-book gentility'(1982,

1). But not only is this a misrepresentation of what women were actually doing in this period, it also implicitly assumes that the interesting writers were self-consciously 'new' and aggressively political.

In fact, between the wars, some women were writing in 'new' ways, in a modernist or feminist sense, while others used older traditions in new ways. It is helpful, too, to keep as open a mind as possible about the nature of 'Scottishness' in writing. Women writers often wrote from an overtly 'Scottish' perspective, which allowed them access to a literary marketplace where Scottish material was in demand and published by firms such as Hodder and Stoughton and John Murray. The 'vernacular' poets such as Violet Jacob, Marion Angus and Helen B. Cruickshank are an interesting case in point: they are often seen as being critically significant because they influenced Macdiarmid, the assumption being that MacDiarmid developed something new and exciting that went beyond their more conventional poetry. However, their poetry has a wider range than has been recognised and can also be seen as exciting in itself. Rooted in the communal ballad and folk song traditions, it uses Scots vernacular to explore many aspects of female experience, including anger and desire. Nostalgic though their poetry may be at times, it can be powerful and suggestive: there are surely more ways than one to read Angus's lines, 'Love, come kiss me/Whaur the twa burns rin' ('Invitation'). This poetry takes for granted that women's experience is important. Catherine Kerrigan suggests that while much women's poetry is concerned with 'isolation and need for self-determination', there is often a confidence in poetry by Scottish women that can be attributed to an older 'female voice of the ballad tradition', a sense women have of being backed up by a 'whole chorus of similar voices [which] preceded them' (1991, 8).

Other kinds of writing also places women's experience unproblematically at the centre of culture; for example the work of twentieth century ethnologists such as F. Marian MacNeill and I. F. Grant, poised as it is somewhere between fiction and cultural history. Agnes Mure Mackenzie looks anew at the myth of Mary, Queen of Scots. Women autobiographers such as Helen B. Cruickshank and Annie S. Swan construct different versions of the relationship between culture and self from those of their male contemporaries. Women dramatists such as Agnes Adam and Ena Lamont Stewart and others (see entry for Adam) were active in the local theatre movement in Glasgow, and use yet another kind of 'Scottishness' to create community and a sense of local identity.

In 1983 it was still possible to claim that the 'Scottish novel is a man-made creation' (Bold, 218). But now, with knowledge of the variety of fiction published by Dorothy K. Haynes, Lorna Moon and others listed below, in addition to the writers whose works are explored in detail in this collection, such a view is no longer tenable.

Works Cited

Bold, Alan *Modern Scottish Literature*. London: Longman, 1983.
Elliot, Robert 'Women, Glasgow and the Novel'. *Chapman*. vol.7. no.3. Autumn 1982, 1–4
Kerrigan, Catherine *An Anthology of Scottish Women Poets*. Edinburgh: Edinburgh University Press, 1991

Select Bibliography

The authors are listed alphabetically under the name they used for publication; their works are listed chronologically. The works listed are those published between 1920 and 1970 with a few exceptions.

Agnes Adam, playwright, perhaps the most prolific among a range of women playwrights (including Barbara Dickson, Edith B. Hannah, Christine Orr, Margaret Wait, Katherine Blair, Marjorie Laws and Eliza Susannah Boswell). She wrote over sixty comedies (predominantly one-act) which were published and acted in Glasgow, in the series 'Scottish Plays' (which also published Joe Corrie), all published by Glasgow: Brown, Son & Ferguson. Adam's very popular plays, mainly acted by women in Scots dialect, satirise class, prejudice and the hierarchies that exist among groups of women. Her one act plays include: *Well-Connected*. 1937, no. 89; *The New Hall*. 1938, no. 96; *A Great Occasion*, [1951], no.147; *China Dogs*. [1952?], no.148; *Forbid Them Not*. 1954, no.163; *Between Two Thieves*. [1955?], no.8; *I Bequeath*. [1960?], no.5; *House of Shadows*. [1963?], no.189; *The Lum Hat*. [1961?], no.187; *Paddy Muldoon's Ghost*. [1964?], no.191; *The Strawberry*. [1965?], no.192; *A Pearl of Great Price*. [1965?], no. 194; *Still Waters*. [1966?], no.197; *Miss Primrose's Husband*. [1966?], no.199. Her three act plays include: *Aunt Janet*. 1946; *Dow's Doughhnuts*. 1953; *Community Centre*. 1955; *Coronets and Cows*. 1960; *Happy Families*. 1962; *Sunshine Susie*.1963.

Hannah Aitken (1911–77), fiction and nonfiction writer, wrote rather dark, retrospective explorations of Scottish childhood, as well as editing a collection of folktales. *In A Shaft of Sunlight*. London: Hodder and Stoughton, 1947. *Whittans*. London: Hodder and Stoughton, 1951. *Seven, Napier Place*. London: Hodder and Stoughton, 1952. *Music for the Journey*. London: Hodder and Stoughton, 1957; *A Forgotten Heritage. Original Folk Tales of Lowland Scotland* ed. Edinburgh: Scottish Academic Press, 1973.

Dot Allan (1892–1964), novelist, contributed to the development of urban realism, many of her novels exploring deteriorating social conditions during economic depression. Allan's dark and often angry fiction challenges the idea that women did not write political novels; it explores class, politics and culture directly. *Hunger March*, for example, is a disturbing novel about a hunger march in June 1933 by unemployed men and women. *The Syrens*. London: William Heinemann, 1921; *Makeshift*. London: Melrose and Co, [1928]; *The Deans*. London: Jarrold, [1929]; *Deepening River*. London: Jarrold, 1932; *Hunger March*. London: Hutchinson, [1934]; *Virgin Fire: The Story of Marion Bradfute*. London: Hutchinson, [1935]; *John Matthew, Papermaker*. London: Hodder and Stoughton, [1948]; *The Passionate Sisters*. London: Robert Hale, 1955; *Charity Begins at Home*. London: Robert Hale, [1958].

Marion E. Angus (1866–1946), poet. Vernacular poetry, revived in the early twentieth century by Violet Jacob and others, is interestingly developed by Angus who evolved ambiguous poetic voices, giving a sense of the intimate and numinous in her poetry. *The Lilt and Other Verses*. Aberdeen: D. Wyllie and Sons, 1922; *The Tinker's Road and Other Verses*. Glasgow: Gowans & Gray, 1924; *Sun & Candlelight*. Edinburgh: Porpoise Press, 1927; *The Singin' Lass*. Edinburgh: Porpoise Press, 1929; *The Turn of the Day*. Edinburgh: Porpoise Press, 1931; *Lost Country, and Other Verses* Glasgow: Gowans & Gray, 1937; *Selected Poems of Marion Angus*. With an introduction by Maurice Lindsay (also ed.) and a personal memoir by Helen B. Cruickshank. Edinburgh: Serif Books, 1950.

Mary Cleland (pseudonym of Margaret Barbour Wells), novelist. She produced several middle-class urban realist novels, with some exploration of class difference. *The Silver Whistle*. London: Heath Cranton, [1920]; *The Two Windows*. London: Hodder & Stoughton, [1922]; *The Sure Traveller*. London: Hodder & Stoughton, [1923]; *The Forsaken Way*. London: Hodder & Stoughton, 1927.

Helen Burness Cruickshank (1886–1975), poet and cultural activist. She contributed to the Scottish Renaissance as founder and secretary for the Scottish P.E.N., 1927-34. In her *Octobiography* she constructs herself as a woman poet and adventurer, with a distinctive sense of her own 'Scottishness'. She wrote both in English and Scots; her vernacular work such as 'Glenskenno Wood' can be haunting. *Up the Noran Water and Other Scots Poems.* London: Methuen & Co., 1934; *Sea Buckthorn.* Dunfermline: H. T. Macpherson, 1954; *The Ponnage Pool.* Edinburgh: Macdonald, 1968; *Collected Poems.* Edinburgh: Reprographia, 1971; *Octobiography.* Montrose: Standard Press, 1976; *More Collected Poems.* Edinburgh: Gordon Wright, 1978.

O. Douglas (pseudonym of Anna Buchan) (1877-1948), popular novelist who wrote middle class domestic fiction and was widely read throughout this period; much of her work, fiction included, was autobiographical in origin. Her writing was all published London: Hodder & Stoughton and included *Penny Plain.* 1920; *Ann and her Mother.* 1922; *The Day of Small Things.* 1930; *The House That Is Our Own.* 1940. As Anna Buchan, she published *Unforgettable, Unforgotten.* 1945; *Farewell to Priorsford.* 1950.

Catherine Irvine Gavin (b.1907), contemporary and historical novelist, explores the effect of economic depression on relationships in her *Clyde Valley*, a novel of female development during a period of social upheaval. She also wrote biographies and on France. Her novels include: *Clyde Valley.* London: Arthur Barker, 1938; *The Hostile Shore.* London: Methuen & Co., 1940; *The Black Milestone.* London: Methuen & Co., 1941; *Madeleine.* London: Macmillan & Co., 1958; *The Cactus and the Crown.* London: Hodder & Stoughton, 1962; *The Fortress.* London: Hodder & Stoughton,1964; her non fiction titles include: *Louis Philippe, King of France.* London: Methuen & Co., 1933; *Edward the Seventh.* London: Jonathan Cape, 1941; *Britain and France: the Entente Cordiale.* London: Jonathan Cape, 1941; *Liberated France.* London: Jonathan Cape, 1955.

I. F. Grant (Isabel Frances)(1887-1983), ethnographer and economic historian; one of the first modern women ethnographers of the Highlands, Grant attempts to reconstruct the 'life of the folk', a tradition from which she sees herself descended; her work creates an unusual intersection of history and autobiography, implying an elevation of experiential authority above that of a more academic kind. *Every-day Life on an Old Highland Farm, 1769-1782.* London: Longman & Co., 1924; *The Social and Economic Development of Scotland before 1603.* Edinburgh: Oliver & Boyd, 1930; *In the Track of Montrose.* London: A. MacLehose & Co., 1931; *Everyday Life in Old Scotland.* London: G.Allen & Unwin, [1932]; *The Economic History of Scotland.* London: Longmans, Green & Co., 1934;

The Macleods: the History of a Clan 1200–1956. London: Faber & Faber, 1959; *Highland Folk Ways*. London: Routledge & Kegan Paul, 1961.

Dorothy Kate Haynes (1918–87), short story writer whose supernatural and fantastic fiction is often darkly psychological, exploring the fears of childhood and focusing on some dark moments of Scottish history: 'The Head' begins with a thief being tortured publicly in downtown Edinburgh. *Winter's Traces*. London: Methuen & Co., 1947; 'The Gibsons of Glasgow' in *Triad Two*. Jack C.R.Aistrop ed. London: Dennis Dobson & Co., 1947; *Thou Shalt Not Suffer a Witch and Other Stories*. London: Methuen & Co., 1949 and Edinburgh: B & W Publishing, 1996; *Robin Ritchie*. London: Methuen & Co, 1949; *Peacocks and Pagodas: the Best of Dorothy K. Haynes*. Edinburgh: Harris, 1981.

Marion Cleland Lochhead (1902–85), vernacular poet adopting a variety of poetic personae: 'But, aince atween the mirk an' licht / I went, whar nae een saw me,' states the speaker of 'Daft Meg's Song'. Lochhead also wrote poetry in English, including some devotional verse, and published ethnographic studies, as well as three novels. *Poems*. London and Glasgow: Gowans & Gray, 1928; *Painted Things, and Other Poems*. London and Glasgow: Gowans & Gray, 1929; *Anne Dalrymple*. Edinburgh: Moray Press, 1934; *Cloaked in Scarlet*. Edinburgh: Moray Press, 1935; *Feast of Candlemas and other Devotional Poems*. Edinburgh: Moray Press, 1937; *The Dancing Flower*. Edinburgh, Moray Press, 1938. *Fiddlers Bidding*. Edinburgh: Oliver and Boyd, 1939; *The Scots Household in the Eighteenth Century*. Edinburgh: Moray Press, 1948; *The Victorian Household*. London: John Murray, [1964].

Bessie Jane Bird MacArthur (b.1889), poet. As well as some highly evocative, rhythmic poetry, MacArthur also wrote at least two 'Celtic plays'; *The Clan of Lochlann* is a strange tale of a half-human woman from the other world who is lured back to the sea; it won the Scots Radio Drama Competition in 1926–27. *The Clan of Lochlann and Silis: Two Celtic Plays*. Edinburgh: W. M. Urquhart & Son, 1928; *The Starry Venture, and Other Poems*. London: E. Matthews & Marrot, 1930; *Scots Poems*. Edinburgh: Oliver and Boyd, 1938; *Last Leave*. Edinburgh: Oliver & Boyd, 1943; *From Daer Water. Poems in Scots and English*. Dunfermline: H.T.Macpherson, 1962; *And Time Moves On*. W. Linton: Castlelaw Press, 1970.

Agnes Mure Mackenzie (1891–1955), historian and novelist; Mackenzie was deeply involved with the Saltire Society's attempt to promote Scottish culture. She wrote both historical fiction and non-fiction, as well as producing some of Scotland's earliest feminist and cultural criticism. Her many works include *Without Conditions*. London: William Heinemann, 1923;

The Women in Shakespeare's Plays: A Critical Study from the Dramatic and the Psychological Points of View and in Relation to the Development of Shakespeare's Art. London: William Heinemann, 1924; *The Quiet Lady*. London: William Heinemann, 1926; *Lost Kinnellan*. London: William Heinemann, 1927; *The Process of Literature: An Essay towards some Reconsiderations*. London: G. Allen & Unwin, 1929; *Between Sun and Moon*. London: Constable & Co.,1932; *An Historical Survey of Scottish Literature*. London: A. Maclehose & Co, 1933; *The Foundations of Scotland*. London and Edinburgh: W.& R. Chambers, 1938; *The Kingdom of Scotland. A Short History*. London and Edinburgh: W.& R.Chambers, 1940.

McNeill, Florence Marian (1885–1973), ethnologist; McNeill's ethnological writing is linked to a larger Scottish cultural/literary tradition. Her *The Scots Kitchen*, among other works, constructs national identity as firmly rooted in the domestic sphere. *The Scots Kitchen; Its Traditions and Lore, with Old-Time Recipes*. London and Glasgow: Blackie & Son, 1929; *The Road Home. A Novel*. London: A. Maclehose, 1932. *The Book of Breakfasts, with Menus, Recipes and Breakfast Lore*. London: A. Maclehose, 1932.*The Scots Cellar: its Traditions and Lore*. Edinburgh: Richard Paterson, 1956; *The Silver Bough. A Study of the National and Local Festivals of Scotland*. 4 vols. Glasgow: William MacLellan, 1957–64.

Lorna Moon (pseudonym of Helen Nora Wilson Low) (1886–1930), fiction and script writer; Moon's career as a Hollywood scriptwriter, following early life in north east Scotland, was cut short by her death from tuberculosis. She wrote some powerful short stories and her novel, *Dark Star* is a female novel of development with a Gothic tone and setting. *Doorways in Drumorty*. London: Jonathan Cape, 1926 and Aberdeen: Gourdas House, 1981; *Dark Star*. London: Victor Gollancz, 1929 and Aberdeen: Gourdas House, 1980; *Too Gay! (Lipstick Lady)*. Newcastle under Lyme: Clifford Lewis, [1945].

Jean Plaidy (pseudonym of Eleanor Alice Burford Hibbert) (b.1906), historical novelist; Plaidy was so prolific in producing historical novels that Alan Bold calls her an 'industry in her own right' (*Modern Scottish Literature*, 1983, 215). Her writing is of varied quality, and her fictionalising of much women's history ranges from the romanticised to strangely speculative. She also wrote under Eleanor Burford. Her works include *Beyond the Blue Mountains*. London: Robert Hale, 1948; *The Italian Woman*. London: Robert Hale, 1952; *Daughter of Satan*. London: Robert Hale, 1952. *Flaunting Extravagant Queen*. London: Robert Hale, 1957; *Katharine, The Virgin Widow*. London: Robert Hale, 1961; *The Haunted Sisters*. London: Robert Hale, 1966.

Ena Lamont Stewart (b.1912), playwright; Stewart produced a range of socially-inspired plays mainly for Glasgow's Unity Theatre, a company founded in 1941 by working-class Glaswegians; like Joe Corrie, she felt that professional theatre had become increasingly less representative of the people; *Men Should Weep* explores power and authority in the domestic sphere of the thirties and has been acted and republished by the theatre company 7:84 Scotland. *Starched Aprons. 1945*; Glasgow: Scottish Society of Playwrights, 1976; *Men Should Weep.* 1947; Edinburgh: 7:84 Publications, 1983, 1986 (with introduction and notes); *The Heir to Ardmally.* 1958.

Annie S. Swan (1859–1943), popular and prolific novelist. She began publishing in 1883 and continued till her death in 1943. She is best known for her 'Kailyard' writing but also wrote novels of middle class life and romances. A selection of her works after 1920 are *Closed Doors.* London and Dundee: J. Leng, 1926; *The Pendulum.* London: Hodder & Stoughton, 1926; *The Last of the Laidlaws. A Romance of the Borders.* London and Dundee: J. Leng, 1933; *My Life. An Autobigraphy.* London: Nicholson & Watson, 1934; *The Land I Love.* London: Nicholson & Watson.

Josephine Tey (pseudonym of Elizabeth Mackintosh) (1896–1952), novelist and playwright; prolific and extremely varied writer. As Josephine Tey, she published a variety of highly readable detective novels; her detectives, both female and male, are intuitive and full of common sense. *Singing Sands* is the only novel set in Scotland. As Gordon Daviot, she published historical novels and plays: *Kif: An Unfinished History.* London: Ernest Benn, 1929; *The Man in the Queue.* London: Methuen, 1929; *The Expensive Halo.* London: Ernest Benn, 1931. *Richard of Bordeaux.* London: Victor Gollancz, 1933; *Queen of Scots.* London: Victor Gollancz, 1934; *Leith Sands, and Other Short Plays.* London: Duckworth, 1946; *The Privateer.* London: Peter Davis, 1952. As Josephine Tey: *A Shilling For Candles.* London: Methuen, 1936; *Miss Pym Disposes.* London: Peter Davies, 1946; *The Franchise Affair.* London: Peter Davies, 1948; *Brat Farrar.* London: Peter Davies, 1948; *To Love and To Be Wise.* London: Peter Davies, 1950; *The Daughter of Time.* London: Peter Davies, 1951; *The Singing Sands.* London: Peter Davies, 1952.

Further Reading

Please refer also to 'Works Cited' at the end of the introduction and individual essays for other bibliographical details.

Catherine Carswell

Small, Christopher Engagement and Detachment, *Chapman*. no.74–5 Autumn/Winter, 1993, 131–6

McCulloch, Margery Palmer 'Women, Carswell and the Scottish Renaissance', *Proceedings of the Scottish Workshop...E.S.S.E Conference...1993', Études Écossaises, special issue.* Horst W. Drescher and Pierre Morère, eds. G.D.R. *Études Écossaises,* Université Stendhal/Scottish Studies Centre, J. Gutenberg-Universität Mainz: Grenoble/Germersheim, 1994, 93–104

Norquay, Glenda 'Catherine Carswell: *Open the Door!'* in *History of Scottish Women's Writing.* Douglas Gifford and Dorothy McMillan eds. Edinburgh: Edinburgh University Press, 1997, 389–99

Jessie Kesson

Adair, Elizabeth *North East Folk*. Edinburgh: Paul Harris, 1982, 78–81

Anderson, Carol 'Listening to the Women Talk' in *The Scottish Novel Since the Seventies.* Gavin Wallace and Randall Stevenson eds. Edinburgh: Edinburgh University Press, 1993, 170–86

Hendry, Joy 'Jessie Kesson Country', *The Scots Magazine.* October 1989, 11–2

Kesson, Jessie 'My Scotland', *The Scottish Review.* vol. 35. 1984, 39–41

Macpherson, Hugh 'Scottish Writers: Jessie Kesson', *Scottish Book Collector.* vol. 8. 1990–1, 22–5

Murray, Isobel 'Jessie Kesson' in *History of Scottish Women's Writing.* Gifford and McMillan, eds. Edinburgh: EUP, 1997, 481–93

Naomi Mitchison

Benton, Jill *Naomi Mitchison: A Biography*. London: Pandora Press, 1990

Dickson, Beth 'From Personal to Global: The Fiction of Naomi Mitchison', *Chapman*. vol.10. Summer 1987, 34–40

Calder, Jenni *The Nine Lives of Naomi Mitchison*. London: Virago, 1997

Calder, Jenni 'More than Merely Ourselves: Naomi Mitchison' in *History of Scottish Women's Writing*. Gifford and McMillan eds. Edinburgh: EUP, 1997, 444–55

Gifford, Douglas 'Forgiving the Past: Naomi Mitchison's *The Bull Calves*' in *Studies in Scottish Fiction: Twentieth Century*. Horst Drescher and Joachim Schwend eds. Frankfurt am Main: Peter Lang, 1990, 219–41

Henegan, Alison 'Alison Henegan talking with Naomi Mitchison' in *Writing Lives: Conversations between Women Writers*. Mary Chamberlain ed. London: Virago, 1988, 170–80

Mitchison, Naomi *You May Well Ask: A Memoir 1920–1940*. 1979; London: Fontana, 1986

Murray, Isobel 'Human Relations: An Outline of Some Major Themes in Naomi Mitchison's Adult Fiction' in *Studies in Scottish Fiction: Twentieth Century*. Horst Drescher and Joachim Schwend eds. Frankfurt am Main: Peter Lang, 1990, 243–56

Plain, Gill *Women's Fiction of the Second World War: Gender, Power and Resistance*. Edinburgh: Edinburgh University Press, 1996, 139–65

Smith, Donald 'You May Well Ask: Nine Decades of Mitchison', *Cencrastus*. vol.13. Summer 1983, 14–7

Nancy Brysson Morrison

There is nothing substantial on Morrison as yet

Willa Muir

Butter, P.H. 'Willa Muir: Writer' in *Edwin Muir: Centenary Assessments*. C.J.M. MacLachlan and D.S.Robb eds. Aberdeen: Association for Scottish Literary Studies, 1988, 58–74

Elphinstone, Margaret 'Willa Muir: Crossing the Genres' in *History of Scottish Women's Writing*. Douglas Gifford and Dorothy McMillan eds. Edinburgh: EUP, 1997, 400–15

Mudge, Patricia Rowland 'A Quorum of Willas', *Chapman*. no.71. special edition 'Peerie Willa Muir'. Winter 1992–3, 1–7. See also other articles mainly of biographical interest in this edition.

Muir, Willa *Living with Ballads*. London: Hogarth, 1965

Manning, Susan ' "Belonging with Edwin": Writing the History of Scottish Women Writers', *Scottish Literary Journal*. Supplement no. 48. Spring 1998, 1–9

Murray, Isobel 'Selves, Names and Roles: Willa Muir's *Imagined Corners* Offers Some Inspiration for *A Scots Quair*'. *Scottish Literary Journal*. vol. 21. May 1994, 56–64

Nan Shepherd

Cullen, Mairi-Ann 'Creating Ourselves: the Poetry of Nan Shepherd', *Chapman*. vol.74–5. Autumn/Winter 1993, 115–8

Manning, Susan ' "Belonging with Edwin": Writing the History of Scottish Women Writers', *Scottish Literary Journal*. Supplement no.48. Spring 1998, 1–9

Watson, Roderick ' To Know Being : Substance and Being in the Work of Nan Shepherd' in *History of Scottish Women's Writing*. Gifford and McMillan eds. Edinburgh: EUP, 1997, 416–27

Muriel Spark

Bold, Alan ed. *Muriel Spark: An Odd Capacity for Vision*. London: Vision, 1984

Bold, Alan *Muriel Spark*. London: Methuen, 1986

Carruthers, Gerard 'The Remarkable Fictions of Muriel Spark' in *History of Scottish Women's Fiction*. Gifford and McMillan eds. Edinburgh: EUP, 1997, 514–25

Little, Judy *Comedy and the Woman Writer: Woolf, Spark and Feminism*. Lincoln, Nebraska: University of Nebraska Press, 1983

Randisi, Jennifer Lynn *On Her Way Rejoicing: the Fiction of Muriel Spark*. Washington, D.C.: Catholic University of America Press, 1991

Rankin, Ian 'The Deliberate Cunning of Muriel Spark' in *The Scottish Novel Since the Seventies*. Gavin Wallace and Randall Stevenson eds. Edinburgh: Edinburgh University Press, 1993, 41–53

Shaw, Valerie 'Muriel Spark' in *The History of Scottish Literature: Volume 4, Twentieth Century*. Cairns Craig ed. Aberdeen: Aberdeen University Press, 1987, 277–90

Rebecca West

Deakin, Motley *Rebecca West*. Boston: Twayne,1980
Ferguson, Moira 'Feminist Manicheanism: Rebecca West's Unique Fusion' in *Minnesota Review*. vol 15. 1980, 53–60
Packer, Joan Garrett *Rebecca West: An Annotated Bibliography*. New York: Garland,1991
Scott, Bonnie Kime 'Refiguring the Binary, Breaking the Cycle: Rebecca West as Feminist Modernist', *Twentieth Century Literature*. vol.37. no.2 1991, 169–91
Scott, Bonne Kime 'The Strange Necessity of Rebecca West' in *Women Reading Women's Writing*. Sue Roe ed. Sussex: Harvester Press, 1987
West, Rebecca *Black Lamb and Grey Falcon*. 1941; Edinburgh: Canongate, 1993
West, Rebecca *The Fountain Overflows*. 1956; Harmondsworth: Penguin, 1985
West, Rebecca *The Young Rebecca: Writings of Rebecca West 1911–1917*. Jane Marcus ed. 1982; London: Virago Press, 1983
Wolfe, Peter *Rebecca West: Artist and Thinker*. Carbondale: Southern Illinois University Press, 1971

Various Authors

Anderson, Carol 'North and South: Scotland, Sex and Otherness' in *La Europa (Cultural) de los Pueblos: Voz Y Forma*. Federico Eguiluz, Elspeth Graham et al eds. Vitoria: University of the Basque Country, 1994, 101–7 (Carswell and West)
Craig, Cairns *The Modern Scottish Novel: Narrative and the National Imagination*. Edinburgh: Edinburgh University Press, 1999
Montefiore, Janet *Men and Women Writers of the 1930s: The Dangerous Flood of History*. London: Routledge, 1996 (Mitchison and West)
Murray, Isobel and Bob Tait, *Ten Modern Scottish Novels*. Aberdeen: Aberdeen University Press, 1984
Norquay, Glenda ' "Welcome, oh mine own rugged Scotland!" Gender and Landscape in Scottish Fiction' in *La Europa (cultural) de los Pueblos:*

Voz Y Forma. Federico Eguiluz, Elspeth Graham et al eds., 1994, 11–31 (Carswell, Kesson and others)

Thomson, David Cleghorn ed. *Scotland in Quest of Her Youth.* Edinburgh: Oliver and Boyd, 1932 (Carswell and Mitchison)

Whiteford, Eilidh M. *Dislodging the Goal-posts and Blowing the House Down: Cultural Authority, National Identity, and Three Women Writers.* Unpublished M.A.Thesis. Guelph, Ontario: University of Guelph, 1993 (West, Carswell and Muir)

See also *A History of Scottish Women's Writing.* Douglas Gifford and Dorothy McMillan eds. Edinburgh: Edinburgh University Press, 1997 for general essays which include references to the authors.

Scotland

Craig, Cairns. *Out of History: Narrative Paradigms in Scottish and English Culture.* Edinburgh: Polygon, 1996

Hagemann, Susanne. '"Bidin' Naiturall": Identity Questions in Scottish Twentieth Century Renaissance Literature', *Scottish Literary Journal.* vol.21. May 1994, 44–5

Rubenstein, Jill. 'Scottish Fiction and the Foreign Reader: Some Reflections', *Scottish Literary Journal* 20. Nov 1993, 86–91

Women and Scotland

Anderson, Carol. 'Debatable Land: The Prose Work of Violet Jacob' in *Tea and Leg-Irons: Feminist Readings from Scotland.* Caroline Gonda ed. London: Open Letters, 1992, 31–44

Anderson, Carol and Glenda Norquay. 'Superiorism', *Cencrastus.* vol.15. Winter, 1984, 8–10

Breitenbach, Esther and Eleanor Gordon eds. *Out of Bounds: Women in Scottish Society 1800–1945.* Edinburgh: Edinburgh University Press, 1993

Breitenbach Esther and Eleanor Gordon eds. *'The World is Ill-Divided': Women's Work in Scotland in the 19th and early 20th centuries.* Edinburgh: Edinburgh University Press, 1992

Burgess, Moira ed. *The Other Voice. Scottish Women's Writing since 1808. An Anthology.* Edinburgh: Polygon, 1987

Freeman, Alan. *'Scotland's Missing Zolas? Fiction by Women 1900–1940'.* Unpublished PhD thesis. Edinburgh: University of Edinburgh, 1994

Elphinstone, Margaret. 'Contemporary Feminist Fantasy in the Scottish Literary Tradition' in *Tea and Leg-Irons: New Feminist Readings from Scotland*. Caroline Gonda ed. London: Open Letters, 1992, 45–59

Glasgow Women's Studies Group. *Uncharted Lives: Extracts from Scottish Women's Experiences, 1850–1982*. Glasgow: Pressgang, 1983

Hendry, Joy. 'The Double Knot in the Peeny' in *In Other Words: Writing as a Feminist*. Gail Chester and Sigrid Nielsen eds. London: Hutchinson, 1987, 37–45

Lochhead, Marion. 'Feminine Quartet', *Chapman: Woven by Women*. vol. 27–8. Summer 1980, 21–31

McMillan, Dorothy Porter. 'Heroines and Writers' in *Tea and Leg-Irons: New Feminist Readings from Scotland*. Caroline Gonda ed. London: Open Letters, 1992, 17–30

Reizbaum, Marilyn. 'Canonical Double Cross: Scottish and Irish Women's Writing' in *Deconstructing Traditions: New Views of Twentieth Century 'British' Literary Canons*. Karen R. Lawrence ed. Urbana, Illinois: University of Illinois Press, 1992, 165–89

Shepherd, Gillian. 'Scottish Women Novelists', *Chapman: Woven by Women*. vol. 27–28. Summer 1980, 50–4

Other

Bell, Ian A. ed. *Peripheral Visions: Images of Nationhood in Contemporary British Fiction*. Cardiff: University of Wales Press, 1995

DuPlessis, Rachel Blau. *Writing Beyond the Ending: Narrative Strategies of Twentieth-Century Women Writers*. Bloomington: Indiana University Press, 1985

Hanscombe, Gillian. *Writing for Their Lives: the Modernist Women 1910–1940*. London: The Women's Press, 1990

Jardine, Alice. *Gynesis: Configurations of Woman and Modernity*. Ithaca: Cornell University Press, 1985

Kaplan, Cora. *Sea Changes: Essays on Culture and Feminism*. London: Verso, 1986

Landry, Donna and Gerald MacLean. *Materialist Feminisms*. Oxford: Blackwell, 1993

Moers, Ellen. *Literary Women*. London: Women's Press, 1977

Newton, Judith and Deborah Rosenfelt eds. *Feminist Criticism and Social Change*. London: Macmillan, 1985

Norquay, Glenda ed. *Voices and Votes: A Literary Anthology of the*

Women's Suffrage Campaign. Manchester: Manchester University Press, 1995

Olsen, Tillie. *Silences*. London: Virago, 1980

Robinson, Lilian. *Sex, Class and Culture*. Bloomington: Indiana University Press, 1978

Sceats, Sarah and Gail Cunningham eds. *Image and Power: Women in Fiction in the Twentieth Century*. London: Longman, 1996

Scott, Bonnie Kime. *Refiguring Modernism, Volume 1: The Women of 1928*. Bloomington and Indianapolis: Indiana University Press, 1995

Showalter, Elaine ed. *The New Feminist Criticism*. London:Virago,1986

Spivak, Gayatri M. *In Other Worlds: Essays in Cultural Politics*. London: Methuen, 1987

Contributors

Carol Anderson has taught Scottish literature at Glasgow University since 1989. Her Ph.D at Edinburgh University was on the representation of women in Scottish fiction. She has edited Violet Jacob's *Diaries and Letters from India 1895–1900*, 1990, and *Flemington and Tales from Angus*, 1998. Her publications include essays on Violet Jacob, Walter Scott, R.L.Stevenson and contemporary Scottish women writers.

Gillian Carter is currently completing her Ph.D thesis, 'Writing Women into Scotland: the Works of Nan Shepherd', at the University of Western Australia. She is a founding editor of the journal, *Outskirts: Feminisms along the Edge* and has published an article in the special 'Celtic Nationalisms' edition of *Span (Journal of the South Pacific Association for Commonwealth Literature and Language Studies)* on women, postcolonialism and nationalism in Scotland.

Aileen Christianson is a senior lecturer in the Department of English literature, Edinburgh University, specialising in nineteenth and twentieth century Scottish literature and women's writing. She has been on the editorial team of the Duke-Edinburgh edition of *The Collected Letters of Thomas and Jane Welsh Carlyle* vols. 1–27, 1970–99, since 1967. Her publications also include essays on Jane Welsh Carlyle, Thomas Carlyle and on twentieth century Scottish women's fiction.

Beth Dickson studied at the universities of St. Andrews and Strathclyde. Her Ph.D focused on Scottish fiction in the first half of the twentieth century. She has published articles on the women writers of this period such as Catherine Carswell and Rachel Annand Taylor and is currently working on issues of literary history. She has recently compiled a study of the fiction of popular novelist, Annie S.Swan.

Margaret Elphinstone is the author of three novels: *The Incomers*, *A Sparrow's Flight*, and *Islanders*, and a collection of short stories *An Apple for a Tree*. She lectures in English studies at Strathclyde University but spent 1997–98 as writer in residence at University of Michigan. She is currently researching on texts by Scottish women writers. She has also published poetry and two books on organic gardening. She has two grown up daughters and lives in Ayrshire.

Alison Lumsden is British Academy research fellow for the Edinburgh edition of the Waverley novels. She is currently co-editing *The Heart of Midlothian* and *Peveril of the Peak*. Her publications include essays on R.L.Stevenson and Alasdair Gray and bibliographies of both the Scottish novel and the Scottish theatre since the seventies.

Isobel Murray is a reader in English at Aberdeen University. With Bob Tait, she co-wrote *Ten Modern Scottish Novels*, 1984. She has edited two collections of the shorter fiction of Naomi Mitchison and written chapters or articles on Jessie Kesson, Grassic Gibbon, Eric Linklater, Mitchison, Robin Jenkins and Willa Muir among others. She edited a long interview with Jessie Kesson in *Scottish Writers Talking*, 1996, and is writing Kesson's authorised biography.

Glenda Norquay is a reader in literature, life and thought at Liverpool John Moores University. Her Ph.D at Edinburgh was on the relationship between Calvinism and realism in nineteenth and twentieth century fiction. She has edited an anthology of writings from the women's suffrage campaign, 1995, and Stevenson's literary and critical essays, 1999. She has published a range of essays on Scottish fiction, particularly Lorna Moon, Catherine Carswell, Mary Brunton and Robin Jenkins.

Margery Palmer McCulloch is currently researching early twentieth-century women writers and their relationship to the Scottish Renaissance. She is the author of *The Novels of Neil Gunn: a Critical Study* and *Edwin Muir: Poet, Critic and Novelist* and the editor of *The Man Who Came Back: Short Stories and Essays by Neil Gunn*. She teaches Scottish literature at the University of Glasgow.

Jennie Rubio was educated at McGill University, Montreal, Quebec, and McMaster, Hamilton, Ontario. She has published an article on Alice Munro and Elspeth Barker in *Scotlands*, 1995; her Ph.D at Edinburgh University was on eighteenth century women's travel writing in Scotland.

Index

This index contains names of people cited in the Introduction and Chapters One to Twelve. Writers who published under pseudonyms are listed under the latter, not their original names. 'Further Reading' and 'Contributors' have not been indexed.

Abel, Elizabeth 14
Accinelli, Letizia 147
Adam, Agnes 159, 160
Aitken, Hannah 161
Allan, Dot 161
Angus, Marion 13, 159, 161
Ardener, Shirley 36
Armour, Jean 152
Arthur, Liz 23
Ashcroft, Bill, Gareth Griffiths and
    Helen Tiffin 55
Auden, W. H. 11

Babha, Homi 39–40
Bakhtin, Mikhail 17, 126–127,
    129
Barrie, J. M. 34
Beethoven, Ludwig von 35
Bergson, Henri 89, 93, 95
Bird, Liz 12
Blair, Katherine 160
Boardman, Philip 29
Boccaccio, Giovanni 20
Bold, Alan 159, 164
Boswell, Eliza Susannah 160
Bronte, Emily 113
Brontes, the 134
Brown, George Douglas 10, 86,
    102–104
Brunton, Mary 11
Buchan, Anna see also Douglas 162
Burford, Eleanor see also Plaidy 164
Burgess, Moira 158
Burkhauser, Jude 25, 27, 30
Burns, Robert 10, 20, 34, 145, 149,
    150, 151, 152, 153, 156
Burrows, Victoria 49

Caird, Janet 96
Caird, Mona 36
Calvin, John 13, 14, 34, 135, 136,
    146

Carswell, Catherine 7, 8, 9, 10, 11,
    13, 14, 15, 17, 20–31, 86, 111, 114
Carswell, Donald 20
Carswell, John 20, 22
Christianson, Aileen 15
Chopin, Kate 41
Cixous, Hélène 17, 27, 48
Clay, Phyllis 22
Cleland, Mary (pseud. of Margaret
    Barbour Wells) 161
Conrad, Joseph 89
Cook, S. A., F. E. Adcock and M. P.
    Charlesworth eds. 74, 82,
Corrie, Joe 160, 165
Craig, Cairns 59, 141
Cruickshank, Helen B. 13, 159,
    161–162

Daviot, Gordon (pseud. of Elizabeth
    Mackintosh; see also Tey) 165
Dickson, Barbara 160
Donaldson, William 150
Donne, John 85
Douglas, O. (pseud. of Anna
    Buchan) 158, 162
Downie, R. A. 75, 82
DuPlessis, Rachel Blau 24, 28

Elliot, Robert 158
Eliot, T. S. 11, 88
Ellis, Havelock 89
Elphinstone, Margaret 15, 27, 28,
    54
Enfantin, B.-P. 94

Felski, Rita 36
Ferrier, Susan 11, 14
Feuchtwangler, Lion 84
Forster, E. M. 89
Fraser, G. S. 150
Frazer, J. G. 11, 74–75, 81, 82,
    87–88, 89

Freud, Sigmund 11, 75, 79, 80, 88, 89, 99

Galloway, Janice 9
Galsworthy, John 89
Gavin, Catherine 162
Geddes, Patrick 24, 29, 30
Gibbon, Lewis Grassic (pseud. of Leslie Mitchell) 13, 84, 108, 130, 147, 150
Gifford, Douglas 8
Gilbert, Sandra M. 11, 17, 37, 114
Gish, Nancy 35
Glendinning, Victoria 34, 42
Gonda, Caroline 8
Graham, Cuthbert 122
Grant, I. F. 159, 162
Grieffenhagen, Maurice 20, 22, 24
Greenham Common Women 126
Grigson, Geoffrey 110
Gubar, Susan 11, 17, 37
Gunn, Neil 11, 13, 46, 108

Hannah, Edith B. 160
Hardy, Thomas 110
Hart, F.R. 11
Haynes, Dorothy K. 9, 159, 163
Hendry, Joy 69
Hewitt, David 59, 147, 148
Hibbert, Eleanor Alice Burford see Plaidy
Hodder and Stoughton 159
Hogg, James 10, 103, 104, 117, 136, 140, 141, 143, 145
Humm, Maggie 16

Ibsen, Henrik 32, 34, 104

Jacob, Violet 13, 14, 159, 161
Jenkins, Alan 135, 136
Jennings, H. F. 30
Joyce, James 21, 35, 87, 89
Jung, Carl 11, 89

Kafka, Franz 84
Keller, Evelyn Fox 48–49, 52
Kemp, Peter 138, 146
Kennedy, A. L. 9
Kermode, Frank 137
Kerrigan, Catherine 158, 159

Kesson, Jessie 8, 9, 10, 11, 12, 13, 14, 15, 16, 46, 120–133, 147–157
Kesson, Johnny 120, 121
Kinchin, Juliet 24, 29, 30
King, Elspeth 12
Kristeva, Julia 17, 40, 41, 60, 62, 63, 64, 67, 70
Lacan, Jacques 79
Lawrence, D. H. 20, 22, 24, 29, 86, 89, 93
Laws, Marjorie 160
Ledger, Sally 37
Leneman, Leah 12
Lindsay, Maurice 11
Lochhead, Marion Cleland 163
Low, Helen Nora Wilson see Moon

MacArthur, Bessie J. B. 163
MacDiarmid, Hugh (pseud. of C. M. Grieve) 11, 13, 35, 46, 118, 150, 152, 153, 159
Macdonald, Frances 24, 26, 30
Macdonald, Margaret 24, 25, 26, 27, 30
Macherey, Pierre 114
Mackenzie, Agnes Mure 46, 159, 163
Mackintosh, Charles Rennie 22, 24, 25, 26, 30
Mackintosh, Elizabeth see Daviot and Tey
McMillan, Dorothy Porter 8
MacNair, Herbert 30
MacNeill, F. Marian 159, 164
Mansfield, Katherine 11
Marcus, Jane 34, 36
Marinetti, Filippo 24
Mary, Queen of Scots 34, 108, 142, 159
Masefield, John 134, 140
Massie, Allan 146
Michie, James 108
Mitchell, Leslie see Gibbon
Mitchison, G. R. 72
Mitchison, Naomi 7, 8, 9, 11, 13, 14, 17, 72–83
Moon, Lorna (pseud. of Helen Nora Wilson Long) 9, 159, 164
Morgan, Edwin 113, 114
Morris, Pam 22, 28, 40, 41, 127, 129
Morrison, Nancy Brysson 7, 8, 9, 11, 13, 14, 15, 16, 17, 108–119

Muir, Edwin 11, 12, 84, 88–89, 108
Muir, Willa 7, 8, 9, 10, 11, 12, 13,
 14, 15, 16, 17, 46, 84–96, 97–106,
 108
Murray, Charles 46
Murray, Isobel 122, 131, 151
Murray, John 159

Neat, Timothy 24, 26
Newbery, Fra 23
Newbery, Jessie 23
Newman, John Henry 134
Norquay, Glenda 146
Norton, Ann 34

Oliphant, Margaret 11, 13, 14
Orel, Harold 40
Orr, Christine 160

Pick, J. B. 11, 87, 89, 95
Pilditch, Jan 24, 29, 30
Plaidy, Jean (pseud. of Eleanor Alice
 Burford Hibbert) 164
Plath, Sylvia 114
Plumwood, Val 51, 55
Pollock, Griselda 36, 37
Pound, Ezra 89
Pykett, Lyn 42

Radford, Mike 121
Raleigh, Walter R. 20
Ray, Philip 33
Rizzio, David 142, 143
Robb, David 101
Robertson, Pamela 26
Rosetti, D. G. 25
Ruskin, John 26
Russo, Mary 131

Said, Edward 99
Saint-Simon, C. -H. 94
Scott, Bonnie Kime 40
Scott, Walter 10, 34, 73, 95, 103,
 104, 117
Shakespeare, William 34, 129, 164
Shelley, Mary 134

Shelley, Percy Bysshe 129
Shepherd, Nan 7, 8, 9, 11, 12, 13,
 14, 15, 16, 46–57, 59–71, 120
Showalter, Elaine 7, 17
Smith, Alison 22, 28, 29, 48
Smith, Donald 11
Sorel, Georges 89
Spark, Muriel 8, 9, 10, 12, 14,
 17, 134–146
Spark, Oswald and Robin 134
Spivak, Gayatri 52
Stallybrass, Peter 126–127, 128
Stevenson, Randall 24, 27
Stevenson, R.L. 10, 34, 103, 104,
 117, 129, 136
Stewart, Ena Lamont 159, 165
Strathern, Christine (pseud. of Nancy
 Brysson Morrison; *see also*
 Morrison) 108
Swan, Annie S. 159, 165

Tey, Josephine (pseud. of Elizabeth
 Mackintosh; *see also* Daviot) 165
Tickner, Lisa 35–36
Torgovnick, Marianna 22, 23, 24,
 27

Vickery, J. 75, 82
Victoria, Queen 33

Wait, Margaret 160
Walker, Lynne 23
Watson, Roderick 47, 48, 67, 122,
 158
Waugh, Patricia 16
Wells, H. G. 32, 42
Wells, Margaret Barbour *see* Cleland
West, Rebecca (pseud. of Cicily Isabel
 Fairfield) 7, 8, 10, 11, 12, 13,
 14, 17, 32–44
White, Allon 126–127, 128
Whyte, Christopher 8, 59
Wolff, Janet 36, 42
Woolf, Leonard 11
Woolf, Virginia 11, 21, 39, 40, 42,
 87, 91, 109, 117